the illustrated
MOVIE QUIZ
book

written & designed by *ROB BURT*   foreword by *BARRY NORMAN*

Rutledge Press
New York, New York

Dedicated to James Robert and Victoria Lea
and in memory of the Regent Cinema, Ely.

Edited and produced by
Severn House Publishers Limited
144-146 New Bond Street
London W1Y 9FD

Published by the Rutledge Press, 112 Madison Avenue,
New York, New York 10016

First printing 1981
Printed in Great Britain

Library of Congress Cataloging in Publication Data

Burt, Robert.
  The illustrated movie quiz book.

  1. Moving-pictures--Miscellanea.
  2. Moving-picture actors and actresses--portraits.
  I. Title.
PN 1993.85.B8 1981 791.43 81-50172
ISBN 0-8317-6112-1 (pbk)   AACR2

Filmset by Filmtype Services Limited, Scarborough
Printed and bound by Morrison & Gibb Limited, Edinburgh

foreword

I t's a quite extraordinary thing – and I don't know whether you've ever noticed it – but *everybody* is an expert on the cinema. The most unlikely people appear in some uncanny way to have total recall not only of every reel of film they ever saw but also of every rolling credit title they ever read.

Ask them any question you like: Who directed the silent version of *Ben Hur*? No, no, too easy. Ask them rather: Who directed the *second unit* on the silent version of *Ben Hur*? They'll know.

As a professional film critic I find these people disconcerting. I am, after all, supposed to be the expert, the acknowledged authority. But far too often I find myself stumped by some amateur movie buff sidling up to me in a pub and laying upon me the kind of poser that nobody should be asked to tackle without at least the prospect of winning a $64,000 prize.

'Here's one for you,' they say. 'How many times did Cecil B. de Mille make *The Squaw Man*?' What kind of daft conundrum is this? How many times can anybody, especially a busy man like de Mille, make the same film? I take a deep breath and suddenly realise that I am surrounded not by one lay-expert but by six – and, unlike me, *they all know the answer.*

What is it about the movies that they should spawn a proliferation of such people? You don't find them in the theatre – at least not to anything like the same extent – and nobody in his right mind is going to watch enough TV to become a television expert. Only in the field of pop music will you find so many self-made experts as you will in the cinema and perhaps that's the answer: pop music and the movies are the popular art forms of this century – they belong to now.

But – and here's an odd thing – every year fewer and fewer people actually go to the cinema. So where do they acquire all this remarkable knowledge? Well, no doubt from TV, whose output depends so heavily on old movies, and of course from books like this. Just flick through this volume and see how cunningly it's arranged.

No matter what species of movie buff, cineaste or lay expert you profess to be – whether past master or eager tyro – there is something here to challenge you. Tackle every quiz here and by the time you've finished what you don't know about the cinema won't be worth knowing anyway. As a professional whose expertise is questioned quite enough already I find the prospect depressing. Indeed, I urged the publishers to suppress the wretched thing but they wouldn't listen to me. Not even on grounds of common humanity.

It's scant consolation, I can tell you, to reflect that whoever you are you won't know nearly as many of the answers as you thought you did and... what? How many times *did* de Mille make *The Squaw Man*? Well, three actually – and that I do know because I've just looked it up.

Barry Norman

The movies, it has been said, are about moments. Golden moments captured forever on celluloid – flickering glimpses of the human condition, sometimes happy, sometimes sad, some good and some not so good, but always memorable.

Just *how* memorable is the concept behind this book. For example, can you name the movie in which **John Wayne** cried 'Fill your hands you son of a bitch', or who originally played **Tarzan,** or how many times and in which movies **Paul Newman** portrayed detective **Lew Harper?**

It's all here in these picture packed pages. Questions about the moments and the people who created them: the players from **Chaplin** to **Nicholson,** the blockbusters from **King Kong** to **Jaws,** the movie makers from **de Mille** to **Truffaut** and many many more – including the answers.

A small but true confession: I have made every effort in my research to acquire the correct birth dates of the screen personalities included. Where reference sources differ I've chosen the kindest.

Rob Burt

Answers: **John Wayne's** quote is from *True Grit* ('69), **Elmo Lincoln** originally played **Tarzan** and **Newman** portrayed **Harper** twice in *Harper* ('66), (GB *The Moving Target*) and *The Drowning Pool* ('75).

quiz guide

Check your answers by looking up the quiz number in the answer section

1 Screen Test

General; worth 2 points each

A   Name the four **Warner Brothers**.
B   How many Oscars did *Mrs Miniver* (*'42*) receive?
C   Who were **The Odd Couple**?
D   Which movie featured **Dirk Bogarde** as a Mexican bandit?
E   Name the major co-stars in the following movies:
  1 *The Producers* (*'68*)
  2 *Gunfight at the OK Corral* (*'57*)
  3 *Midnight Cowboy* (*'69*)
  4 *The Sting* (*'73*)
  5 *You Can't Win 'em All* (*'70*)
F   **Helen Gahagan** took the title role in 1935 and **Ursula Andress** in 1965; name the movies.
G   Who used the hypnotic phrase 'Afghanistan Banana-stand to steal a diamond'?
H   How many trombones led *The Music Man's* (*'62*) big parade?

Flaming Star (see 1 W)

I   Which movie included **Henry Fonda, Natalie Wood, Mel Ferrer, Tony Curtis** and **Lauren Bacall** in the cast?
J   What was **John Wayne's** nationality in *The Sea Chase* (*'55*)?
K   Name the 1977 comedy spoof based on **Alfred Hitchcock's** movies.
L   Who composed the music scores for?
  1 *How to Steal A Million* (*'66*)
  2 *Images* (*'72*)
  3 *Guide For the Married Man* (*'67*)
  4 *Boeing-Boeing* (*'65*)
  5 *The Towering Inferno* (*'74*)
M   **Edward C. Judson, Orson Welles, Aly Khan, Dick Haymes** and **James Hill** were just some of her many real-life husbands, who is she?
N   Name the four sets of brothers who portrayed **The Long Riders** in the film of the same name.
O   Who is **Larry Hagman's** actress mother?
P   For which film did **Elizabeth Taylor** receive her second Oscar?
Q   What was the baby in *Bringing up Baby* (*'38*)?
R   An Egyptian born actor has portrayed many nationalities including a Spanish prince, a Russian doctor and a Mexican killer. By which name has he won international fame and name the movies the characters listed appeared in?
S   Who portrayed New York prostitute **Bree Daniel**?
T   Which film includes a scene in which **Clifton Webb** overturns a bowl of oatmeal over a fractious infant?
U   Who was **Asta's** master?
V   By which name was **Laszlo Loewenstein** better known?
W   Who directed?
  1 *Baby Face Nelson* (*'57*)
  2 *Flaming Star* (*'60*)
  3 *Play Misty for Me* (*'71*)
  4 *Charley Varrick* (*'73*)
  5 *Hell is for Heroes* (*'62*)
X   What was the Great White Shark, star of *Jaws* (*'75*), nicknamed?
Y   Whose singing voice did **Jayne Mansfield** mime to in *The Sheriff of Fractured Jaw* (*'59*)?
Z   Name the three movies in which **Natalie Wood** has appeared with **Robert Redford**.

Film Poster 1 *General; worth 2 points each*
Give the title of the film this poster is advertising.

The Kid (see 2 H)

2 The Players: Charles Chaplin

Specialist; worth 4 points each

A Where and when was he born?
B Which theatrical company did he join in 1907?
C When did he first enter the US?
D Who invited him to join the Keystone Film Company?
E Name his début film.
F Which movie introduced the **Tramp** and who directed it?
G How many movies did he make for the Essanay Company?
H Who portrayed **The Kid** in the film of the same name *('20)*?
I When did he make *Modern Times*?
J Which birthday did he celebrate whilst making *A Countess from Hong Kong ('66)*?

The Big Picture Quiz 1:
King Kong

Specialist; worth 4 points each

A When was it released?
B Who originally conceived the idea?
C What was **Willis O'Brien's** contribution to the movie?
D Name the island on which **Kong** was found.
E Who directed the film?
F What was The Venture?
G Who wrote the screenplay?
H Where did **Kong** meet his end?
I Who portrayed?
   1 **Carl Denham**
   2 **Jack Driscoll**
   3 **Ann Darrow**
   4 **Engelhorn**
J When was the remake released?

3 The Pioneers
Specialist; worth 4 points each

A Who gave Hollywood its name?

B What did the initials **D.W.** in **D.W. Griffith** stand for?

C When (full date) did **Chaplin,**

Pickford, Fairbanks and **Griffith** form the United Artists Corporation?

D Who was labelled 'The man of a thousand faces'?

E By which name was **John Pringle** better known?

F Where did **Douglas Fairbanks Sr** and **Mary Pickford** reside?

G When was the Hollywood sign erected?

H Who was dubbed the 'It girl'?

I Name the players who portrayed **John Wilkes Booth** and **General Grant** in *Birth of a Nation;* when was it released?

J When was the Keystone Company founded and by whom?

K Name **Chaplin's** first movie for United Artists.

L Who once called **Harry Carey** 'the greatest cowboy in pictures'?

M Name **Harry Langdon's** first feature for Warner Brothers.

N Who was once known as **Lonesome Luke**?

O Who directed *Metropolis ('26)*?

P By which name was **Bela Lugosi** originally known?

Q Who directed *Enoch Arden ('11)*?

R By which name was **Wong Liu Tsong** better known?

S Who portrayed **Christ** in **De Mille's** *King of Kings ('27)*?

T What was **Erich von Stroheim's** full name?

U Which comedian was famous for his cross-eyes?

V When was the original *Thief of Baghdad* released?

W As whom did **Reatha Watson** find fame?

X Who portrayed **Min** and **Bill**?

Y Name **William S. Hart's** début movie.

Z Which year saw the release of *The Jazz Singer*?

Mystery Star 1
Clues are set on a diminishing points' scale with (a) worth 5 and (e) worth 1

A Female, born Amarillo, Texas, March 8 1921.

B Joined the **Ballet Russe** in her teens.

C Signed with MGM in 1944.

D Married her second husband **Tony Martin** in 1947.

E Her movies include: *Singin' in the Rain ('52), The Unfinished Dance ('47), Two Weeks In Another Town ('62)* and *The Silencers ('67)*.

Chaplin (see 3 C & K)

The Jazz Singer (see 3 Z)

4 The Players: Rudolph Valentino

Specialist; worth 4 points each

A Where and when was he born?
B What was his full name?
C When did he enter the US?
D Who became his first wife?
E Name the character he portrayed in *The Four Horsemen of the Apocalypse* ('21).
F Who said of him 'His acting is largely confined to protruding his large, almost occult, eyes until the vast areas of white are visible, drawing back the lips of his wide, sensuous mouth to bare his gleaming teeth and flaring his nostrils'?
G When was *The Sheik* released?
H Where and when did he marry **Natacha Rambova**?
I Who on July 18 1923 announced **Valentino** as the first star of Ritz-Carlton Pictures?
J Name his last movie and its director.

Star Couple 1
General; worth 2 points each

Identify this 'on and off' screen couple.

5 Screen Test
General; worth 2 points each

A Who said 'God makes stars, and the public recognises his handiwork'?

B By which name was **Sean O'Fearna** better known?

C Who portrayed the title roles in **Lelouch's** *A Man and A Woman* *('66)*?

D What was the title of the first movie directed by **Peter Bogdanovich**?

E Who in 1960 portrayed **Ferdinand Waldo Demara** and in which movie?

F Name the four actors who have played **James Bond**.

G Who in 1976 asked 'Is it safe?' and in which film was it asked?

H **George Kennedy** had one line in a 1960 **Stanley Kubrick** movie; name the movie and quote the line.

I Who narrated *Zulu ('63)*?

J What have **James T. Pierce, Kamuela C. Searle, Bruce Bennett**

The Public Enemy (see 5 K)

and **Glenn Morris** in common?

K Who received a face-full of grapefruit from **James Cagney** in *The Public Enemy ('31)*?

L Name the 1933 release featuring a naked **Hedy Lamarr**.

M Who gave a memorable performance as the Japanese commander in *The Bridge on the River Kwai ('57)*?

N Where did **Norma Desmond** reside?

O Who in 1945 spent a *Lost Weekend*?

P *Eve knew her Apples ('45)* and *You Can't Run Away From It ('56)* were musical remakes of which 1934 romantic comedy classic?

Q Who was tagged **Duke**?

R Name the film in which **Hayley Mills** received her first screen kiss.

S Which husband and wife team appeared in *From the Terrace ('60)*?

T Who portrayed **Mister Roberts**?

U **Dan Dailey, Richard Conte, Jack Hawkins** and **Vittorio De Sica** co-starred in which TV series?

V By which name was **Harlean Carpentier** better known?

W *The Inn of the Sixth Happiness ('59)* told the story of which famous missionary?

X Name one of the six **Dead End Kids**.

Y Where in 1945 did **Ginger Rogers, Van Johnson, Lana Turner** and **Walter Pidgeon** spend a weekend?

Z Who portrayed the leads in?
1 *In the Heat of the Night ('67)*
2 *In the Cool of the Day ('63)*

Mystery Star 2
Clues are set on a diminishing points' scale with (a) worth 5 and (e) worth 1.

A Male, born Philadelphia Pa., December 9 1910.

B The son of famous theatrical parents.

C Married actress **Kay Griffith** in 1941.

D Starred in the TV series *Highway Patrol (1955–59)*.

E His movies include: *The Runaround ('46), All the King's Men ('50), The Oscar ('66)* and *The Private Files of J. Edgar Hoover ('78)*.

Mystery Star 3

Clues are set on a diminishing points scale with (a) worth 5 and (e) worth 1.

A   Male, born Figeac, France, August 8 1897.
B   Studied acting at the Paris Conservatoire.
C   Arrived in Hollywood in 1929.
D   Gained a reputation as the screen's 'Great Lover'.
E   His movies include *L'Homme du Large* ('20), *Algiers* ('38), *Gaslight* ('44) and *Barefoot in the Park* ('68).

6   Stage Names

Specialist; worth 3 points each

Stage names have always been a stock-in-trade with movie people, many stars choosing a new name in order to enhance their particular image. Others, especially in the not-too-distant past, had their names changed by their studio or agent so as to sound more glamorous or memorable.
By which names are the following better known?

A   **Issur Danielovitch Demsky**
B   **Roy Fitzgerald (Scherer)**
C   **Gladys Smith**
D   **Maurice Micklewhite**
E   **Ivo Levi**
F   **Julia Turner**
G   **Merle Johnson**
H   **Spangler Arlington Brugh**
I   **Richard Jenkins**
J   **Michel Shalhouz**
K   **Alexandra Zuck**
L   **Ira Grossel**
M   **Tula Ellice Finklea**
N   **Charles Buchinski**
O   **Gail Shekles**
P   **Martin Caliniff**
Q   **Paula Ragusa**
R   **Ethel Zimmerman**
S   **Leo Jacoby**
T   **Henry H. McKinnies**
U   **Marion Michael Morrison**
V   **Elke Schletz**
W   **Nathan Birnbaum**
X   **Maureen Fitzsimmons**
Y   **Rosita Dolores Alverio**
Z   **Walter Matasschanskayasky**

Film Poster 2

General; worth 2 points each

Give the title of the film this poster is advertising.

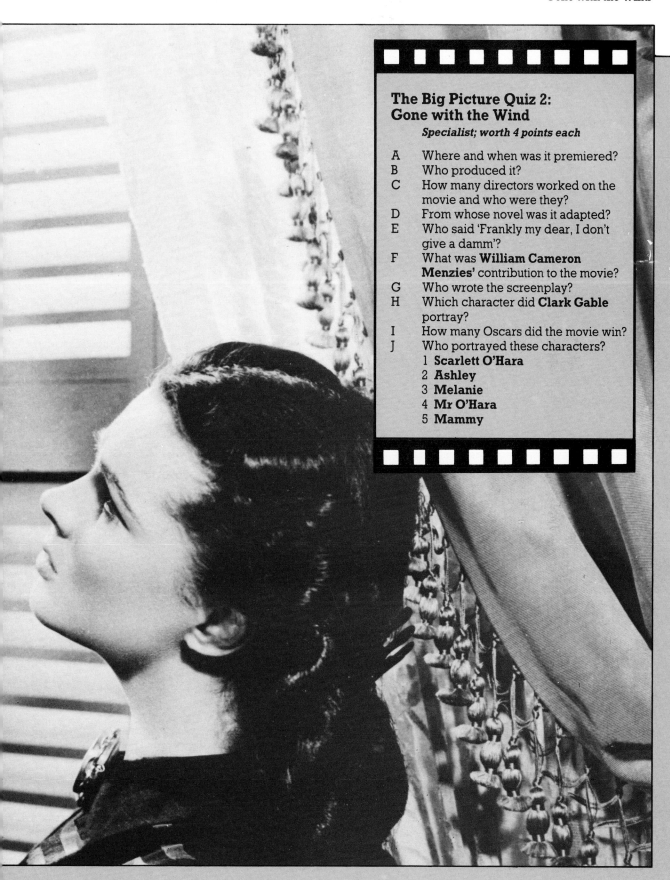

**The Big Picture Quiz 2:
Gone with the Wind**

Specialist; worth 4 points each

A   Where and when was it premiered?
B   Who produced it?
C   How many directors worked on the movie and who were they?
D   From whose novel was it adapted?
E   Who said 'Frankly my dear, I don't give a damm'?
F   What was **William Cameron Menzies'** contribution to the movie?
G   Who wrote the screenplay?
H   Which character did **Clark Gable** portray?
I   How many Oscars did the movie win?
J   Who portrayed these characters?
    1 **Scarlett O'Hara**
    2 **Ashley**
    3 Melanie
    4 **Mr O'Hara**
    5 **Mammy**

7 The Players: Greta Garbo
Specialist; worth 4 points each

A Where and when was she born?
B What was her original name?
C Who in 1924 became her mentor?
D Name her début movie.
E When did she first enter the US?
F Name her first movie with **John Gilbert**?
G Of which film was *Anna Karenina ('35)* the remake?
H Who directed her first talkie and what was its title?
I To whom did she address her most famous line 'I want to be alone'?
J Who accepted her special Oscar in 1954?

8 Screen Test
General; worth 2 points each

A Name **Gummo's** four brothers.

B Where was Rick's American Café situated?

C *Atlantic ('29)* and *A Night to Remember ('58)* told the story of which great disaster?

D Who is **Carol Reed's** actor nephew?

E Name the sisters of the following actresses who have also appeared in movies:
1 **Carmen Miranda**
2 **Brigitte Bardot**
3 **Pier Angeli**
4 **Hayley Mills**
5 **Natalie Wood**

F Which movie featured **Anthony Quinn** in an Oscar winning role as the artist **Gauguin**?

G Who directed *The Swimmer ('68)*?

H Which film won **Peter Finch** his posthumous Oscar?

I Name the stars who ultimately escaped in *The Great Escape ('63)*.

J *The King and I ('56)* was a musical remake of which 1946 Oscar winner?

K Which TV series was based on **George Lucas'** *American Graffiti ('73)*?

L Who portrayed the blind man in **Mel Brooks'** *Young Frankenstein ('74)*?

M Name the major co-stars in the following movies:
1 *Freebie and the Bean ('74)*
2 *Run Silent, Run Deep ('58)*
3 *S.P.Y.S. ('74)*
4 *The War Wagon ('67)*
5 *California Split ('74)*

N By which names were **Frances Gumm** and **Joe Yule** better known?

O In which movie did **Gregory Peck** portray **F. Scott Fitzgerald**?

P Who directed *A Clockwork Orange ('72)*?

Q Name the author of *The Choirboys ('77)* and *The Onion Field ('79)*.

R Which film included **Edward G. Robinson, Richard Widmark, Arthur Kennedy, Gilbert Roland, Carroll Baker** and **James Stewart** in the cast?

S Who portrayed the assassin in **Fred Zinnemann's** *The Day of The Jackal ('73)*?

T In which film did **Sidney Poitier** and **Tony Curtis** appear chained together?

U Name **Beau** and **Jeff's** famous father.

V Who portrayed **Jean Harlow** in the 1965 movie *Harlow*?

W Which famous director wrote a book in praise of the cinema of **Alfred Hitchcock**?

X **Alec Guinness** portrayed a whole family in *Kind Hearts and Coronets ('49)*; what was the family's name?

Y Who led an *Assault on a Queen ('66)*?

Z In *The Adventures of Robin Hood ('38)* who portrayed?
1 **Robin**
2 **Maid Marion**
3 **Prince John**
4 **Guy of Gisbourne**

*Carmen Miranda
(see 8 E)*

9 The Movie Makers: Laurel and Hardy
Specialist; worth 4 points each

A Where and when was **Stan Laurel** born?

B By which name was **Laurel** originally known?

C Where and when was **Oliver Hardy** born?

D In which year did they team up?

E When was **Stan Laurel** awarded a special Academy Award for his creative pioneering in the field of cinema comedy?

Tracy & Hepburn (see 10 G)

10 The Players: Spencer Tracy
Specialist; worth 4 points each

A Where and when was he born?
B What was his full name?
C Name his début movie.
D Who directed his first Hollywood movie?
E What was the title of the first film he made with **Clark Gable**?
F Who did he call the best actress he'd ever worked with 'except one'?
G How many movies did he make with **Katharine Hepburn**?
H Who portrayed **Livingstone** to his **Stanley**?
I Name the 1955 movie he made based on **Don Maguire's** story *Bad Time at Honda*.
J In which movies did he portray the following characters?
   1 **Matt Drayton**
   2 **Father Matthew Doonan**
   3 **Adam Bonner**
   4 **Thomas A. Edison**
   5 **Father Flanagan**

The Wizard of Oz
(see 12 X & Y)

11 Title Roles

General; worth 2 points each

Who portrayed the following characters?

A **Marty**
B **Bob and Carol and Ted and Alice**
C **Sebastian**
D **John and Mary**
E **Camille**
F **Alfie**
G **Pat and Mike**
H **Bonnie and Clyde**
I **Jeremy**
J **Lili**
K **Charly**
L **Robin and Marion**
M **Ben**
N **Candy**
O **Pete 'n' Tillie**
P **Duffy**
Q **Claudia and David**
R **Carrie ('76)**
S **Mame**
T **Cain and Mabel**
U **Joe**
V **David and Lisa**
W **Rocky**
X **Cynthia**
Y **Marnie**
Z **Anna**

12 Screen Test

General; worth 2 points each

A Who directed *M.A.S.H* ('70)?
B Name the actor who shared the car with **Peter Fonda** and **Susan George** in *Dirty Mary, Crazy Larry* ('74).
C Which year saw the release of the **Billie Holiday** bio-pic *Lady Sings the Blues*?
D Who in 1948 portrayed the **Kissing Bandit** in the film of that name?
E Who composed the music for?
   1 *A Man and A Woman* ('66)
   2 *Happy New Year* ('73)
   3 *Bilitis* ('78)
   4 *Day for Night* ('73)
   5 *Live for Life* ('67)
F Which 1974 **Lerner and Loewe** musical featured **Gene Wilder** in the cast?
G Which character did **Brock Peters** portray in *To Kill a Mockingbird* ('63)?
H Who directed *The Wild One* ('54)?
I By which name was **Shirley Schrift** better known?
J Which character have both **Elvis Presley** and **Edward G. Robinson** portrayed?
K Who portrayed **Barnes Wallis** in *The Dam Busters* ('54)?
L Which actress once qualified as a Maine lifeguard?
M In which war were *I Want You* ('51) and *The Hook* ('62) set?
N Name the 1954 movie that teamed **Judy Holliday** and **Jack Lemmon**.
O By which other title was *The Greengage Summer* ('61) known?
P In *The Band Wagon* ('53) who portrayed?
   1 **Tony Hunter**
   2 **Gaby**
   3 **Jeffrey Dordova**
   4 **Lester Marton**
   5 **Lilly Marton**
Q What was the title of the **Bill Naughton** play which was filmed as *The Family Way* ('67)?
R How long was *The Longest Day* ('62)?
S Which character have both **Julie Harris** and **Liza Minnelli** portrayed?
T Who composed the **James Bond** theme?
U Which movie was started in 1940, completed in 1943 but not publicly shown until 1946?
V Who is **Edward Fox's** actor brother?
W By which name was **Diana Dors** originally known?
X In *The Wizard of Oz* ('39) who portrayed?
   1 **Dorothy**
   2 **The Scarecrow**
   3 **The Tin Man**
   4 **The Cowardly Lion**
   5 **The Wizard**
Y Under which title was the seventies remake of *The Wizard of Oz* released?
Z What have **Langhorne Burton, George Curzon, David Farrar** and **Geoffrey Toone** in common?

The Wild One (see 12 H)

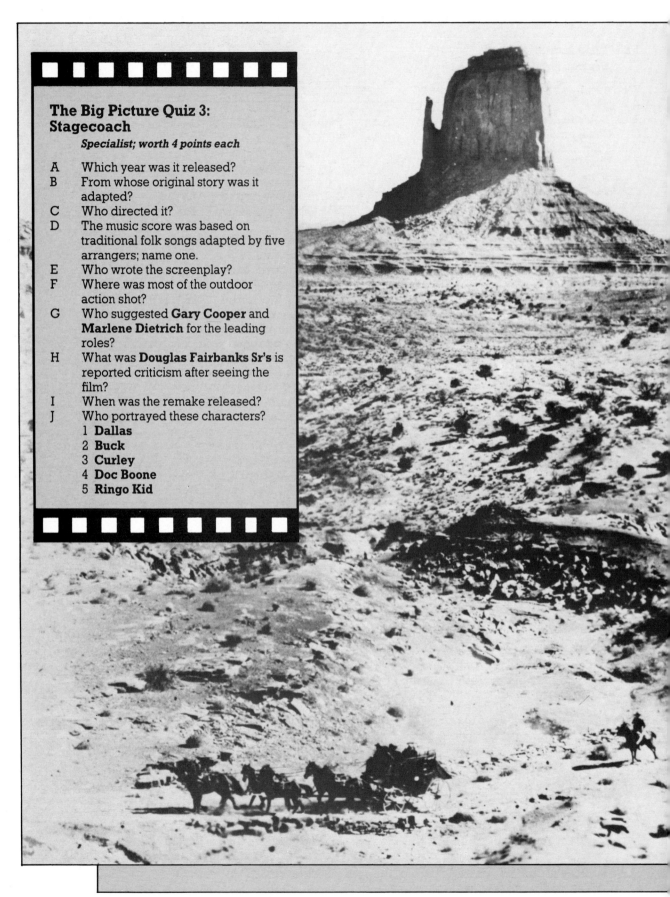

The Big Picture Quiz 3: Stagecoach
Specialist; worth 4 points each

A   Which year was it released?
B   From whose original story was it adapted?
C   Who directed it?
D   The music score was based on traditional folk songs adapted by five arrangers; name one.
E   Who wrote the screenplay?
F   Where was most of the outdoor action shot?
G   Who suggested **Gary Cooper** and **Marlene Dietrich** for the leading roles?
H   What was **Douglas Fairbanks Sr's** is reported criticism after seeing the film?
I   When was the remake released?
J   Who portrayed these characters?
     1 **Dallas**
     2 **Buck**
     3 **Curley**
     4 **Doc Boone**
     5 **Ringo Kid**

13 The Players: Clark Gable
Specialist; worth 4 points each

A Where and when was he born?
B What was his full name?
C Who in 1922 said that **Gable** had 'absolutely nothing to offer, either now or in the future'?
D For which 1934 movie did he receive the Best Actor Academy Award?
E Who called him a 'big ape'?
F When did he marry **Carole Lombard**?

G Which rank did he achieve by the end of World War II?
H Name the first movie he made after being demobbed from the USAF?
I Who directed his last movie and what was its title?
J Name the characters he portrayed in:
1 *Gone With the Wind* ('39)
2 *Mutiny on the Bounty* ('35)
3 *San Francisco* ('36)
4 *Test Pilot* ('38)
5 *Boom Town* ('40)

14 The Movie Makers: Cecil B. de Mille
Specialist; worth 4 points each

A   Where and when was he born?
B   What was his full name?
C   Name his début movie.
D   He formed a production company with two other Hollywood moguls. Who were they?
E   In which movie did he appear as himself?

15 The Movie Makers: Fred Astaire
Specialist; worth 4 points each

A   Where and when was he born?
B   By which name was he originally known?
C   Who was his first dance partner?
D   Name his début movie.
E   In which movie did he perform the 'Carioca' number with **Ginger Rogers**?

16 Screen Test
General; worth 2 points each

A   Who was once labelled 'A female Brando'?
B   Name **James Caan's** début movie.
C   Where was **Julie Christie** born?
D   In which film did **Fred Clark** make his last screen appearance?
E   Who portrayed the ex-**Tarzan** actor in *La Dolce Vita* ('61)?
F   Name the character **William Bendix** portrayed on both radio and television for almost a decade.
G   Who first performed 'Singing in the Rain' on the screen?
H   Which movie marked **Dana Andrews'** screen début?
I   Name the films in which the following actresses portrayed **Queen Elizabeth I**:
 1 **Sarah Bernhardt**
 2 **Lady Diana Manners**
 3 **Flora Robson**
 4 **Bette Davis**
 5 **Jean Simmons**
 6 **Athene Seyler**
J   Which character has been played by **Carlyle Blackwell, Jack Buchanan, Ralph Richardson, Ray Milland, Walter Pidgeon** and **Richard Johnson** amongst others?
K   Who once described himself as a 'sort of everyman's everyman, the perfect middle class type'?
L   Name the animated feature film based on the music of the **Beatles**.
M   Who was **Anne Baxter's** famous grandfather?
N   What nationality was **Stephen Boyd**?
O   In which year was **Disney's** *Pinocchio* released?
P   Who portrayed **Douglas Bader** in *Reach for The Sky* ('56)?
Q   What was **Edgar Buchanan's** original profession?
R   Who directed *Dressed To Kill* ('80)?
S   Name **Yul Brynner's** début movie.
T   In which 1975 movie did **Julie Christie** and **Elliot Gould** feature in cameo roles?
U   Who portrayed **Giovanna Goodthighs** in *Casino Royale* ('67)?
V   In which movie did **Maurice Chevalier** first treat the public to a rendering of 'Every Little Breeze Seems to Whisper Louise'?
W   Name the individual episodes featured in *Story of Three Loves* ('53).
X   Which title did **Dyan Cannon** win in 1955?
Y   Who composed the soundtrack music for?
 1 *Bullitt* ('68)
 2 *Enter the Dragon* ('73)
 3 *Gone With the Wave* ('65)
 4 *The Gauntlet* ('78)
 5 *Dirty Harry* ('71)
Z   Name the actors who have portrayed **Inspector Jacques Clouseau**.

Fred Astaire (see 15)

James Caan (see 16 B)

Julie Christie (see 16 C & T)

*James Cagney
(see 17 E)*

17　The Movie Makers: James Cagney

Specialist; worth 4 points each

A　Where and when was he born?
B　What is his full name?
C　Name his début movie.
D　Which character did he portray in *A Midsummer Night's Dream* ('35)?
E　In which movie did he portray **George M. Cohan?**

Mystery Star 4

Clues are set on a diminishing points' scale with (a) worth 5 and (e) worth 1.

A　Male, born Brooklyn, New York, October 29 1947.
B　Moved to California in 1956 and attended Beverly Hills High School.
C　He acquired an agent at the age of fifteen.
D　Appeared in many TV series including *The Big Valley* and *Mod Squad.*
E　His movies include: *The Young Runaways* ('68), *Hello Down There* ('68); *American Graffiti* ('73) and *Jaws* ('75).

Mystery Star 5

Clues are set on a diminishing points' scale with (a) worth 5 and (e) worth 1.

A　Female, born Tallahassee, Florida, January 14 1941.
B　Christian name **Dorothy**.
C　An original member of the Lincoln Center Repertory Company.
D　One-time wife of rock singer **Peter Wolfe**.
E　Her movies include: *The Happening* ('67), *The Arrangement* ('70), *Little Big Man* ('71) and *The Eyes of Laura Mars* ('78).

18　The Movie Makers: Edward G. Robinson

Specialist; worth 4 points each

A　What was his real name?
B　Where was he born?
C　Name the 1930 gangster movie which gave him star status.
D　What were the titles of the two movies he made under **John Ford's** direction?
E　Which character did he portray in *The Prize* ('64)?

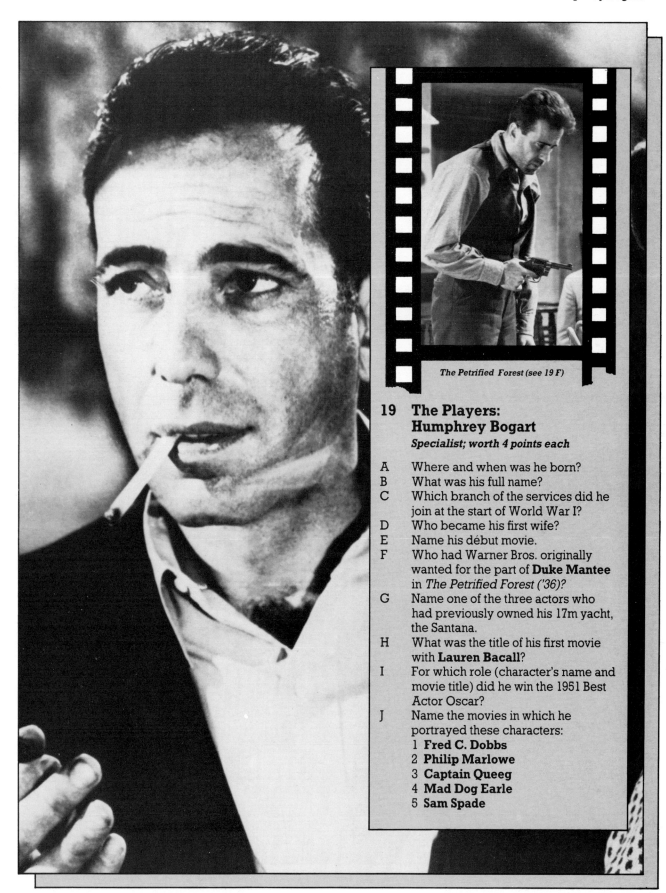

The Petrified Forest (see 19 F)

19 The Players: Humphrey Bogart
Specialist; worth 4 points each

A   Where and when was he born?

B   What was his full name?

C   Which branch of the services did he join at the start of World War I?

D   Who became his first wife?

E   Name his début movie.

F   Who had Warner Bros. originally wanted for the part of **Duke Mantee** in *The Petrified Forest ('36)*?

G   Name one of the three actors who had previously owned his 17m yacht, the Santana.

H   What was the title of his first movie with **Lauren Bacall**?

I   For which role (character's name and movie title) did he win the 1951 Best Actor Oscar?

J   Name the movies in which he portrayed these characters:
1 **Fred C. Dobbs**
2 **Philip Marlowe**
3 **Captain Queeg**
4 **Mad Dog Earle**
5 **Sam Spade**

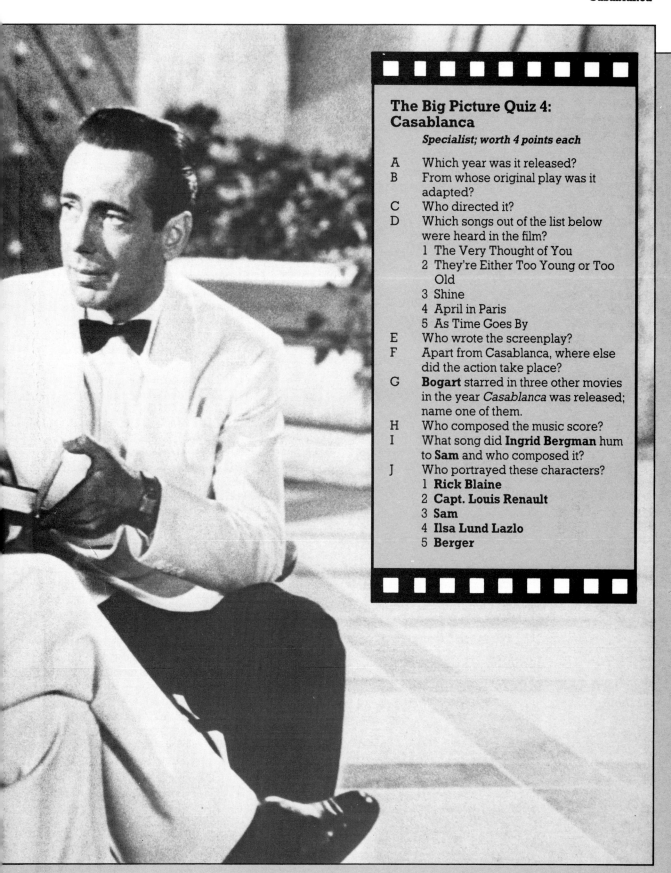

The Big Picture Quiz 4: Casablanca

Specialist; worth 4 points each

A   Which year was it released?

B   From whose original play was it adapted?

C   Who directed it?

D   Which songs out of the list below were heard in the film?
1 The Very Thought of You
2 They're Either Too Young or Too Old
3 Shine
4 April in Paris
5 As Time Goes By

E   Who wrote the screenplay?

F   Apart from Casablanca, where else did the action take place?

G   **Bogart** starred in three other movies in the year *Casablanca* was released; name one of them.

H   Who composed the music score?

I   What song did **Ingrid Bergman** hum to **Sam** and who composed it?

J   Who portrayed these characters?
1 **Rick Blaine**
2 **Capt. Louis Renault**
3 **Sam**
4 **Ilsa Lund Lazlo**
5 **Berger**

Gary Cooper (see 21 E)

20 Stage Names

Specialist; worth 3 points each

By which names are the following better known?

A **Natasha Gurdin**
B **Michael James Vijencio Gubitosi**
C **Allen Stewart Konigsberg**
D **Melvin Kaminsky**
E **Vera Jayne Palmer**
F **Carmen Ricky Orrico**
G **Ernestine Russell**
H **Raquel Tejada**
I **Nicholas Adamschock**
J **Eddie Heimberger**
K **Ella Geisman**
L **Carver Andrews**
M **Cornelius van Mattemore**
N **Donald Robert Smith**
O **Frederick Austerlitz**
P **Betty Jean Perske**
Q **Eugene Klass**
R **Frederick McIntyre Bickel**
S **Shirley Beaty**
T **Derek Van Den Bogaerd**
U **Byron Barr**
V **James Johnson**
W **Randolph Crane**
X **Ann Leppert**
Y **Jill Oppenheim**
Z **Catherine Dorleac**

21 Screen Test

General; worth 2 points each

A Name the individual **Ritz Brothers**.
B Who directed *Belle de Jour ('66)*?
C What was **Crosby, Hope** and

A Summer Place (see 21 M)

Lamour's destination in the first road picture?
D Which 1969 movie directed by **Arthur Penn** was based on a contemporary rock song?

E How many movies did **Gary Cooper** make?
F Name the character portrayed by both **Alan Ladd** and **Steve McQueen**.
G What was **Jason Robards'** occupation in *A Thousand Clowns ('65)*?
H In *Yanks ('80)* who portrayed?
  1 **Matt**
  2 **Jean**
  3 **Helen**
  4 **Danny**
  5 **John**
I By which name was **Beau Bridges** originally known?
J Who was **George Sanders'** actor brother?
K By which name was **Lily Chauchoin** better known?
L In which movie did **Angie Dickinson** portray **Marlon Brando's** screen wife?
M Who composed the music scores for?
  1 *A Summer Place ('59)*
  2 *Parrish ('61)*
  3 *Cash McCall ('60)*
  4 *The Big Sleep ('46)*
  5 *Rome Adventure ('62)*
N Name **Judy Garland's** actress daughter.
O Name the characters **Bette Davis** and **Paul Henreid** portrayed in *Now Voyager ('42)*.
P Name **Gene Hackman's** début movie.
Q For which movie did **Burt Lancaster** win an Academy Award for Best Actor?
R Name the first CinemaScope movie and the inventor of the system.
S By which name was **Alfred Arnold Cocozza** better known?
T For which role is **George Lazenby** famous?
U Who directed *Touch of Evil ('58)*?
V Name the 1945 movie in which **Oscar Levant** portrayed himself.
W Who played the black sheriff in *Blazing Saddles ('74)*?
X Which character did **David McCallum** portray in *The Spy with My Face ('66)*?
Y Who is **Kirk Douglas'** actor producer son?
Z How old was **Sidney Greenstreet** when he made his début movie?

22 The Players: Carole Lombard
Specialist; worth 4 points each

A   Where and when was she born?
B   What was her real name?
C   Name her début movie and the year of its release.
D   What forced her into temporary retirement early on in her career?
E   For whom did she make a series of two-reelers?
F   Who did she marry in 1931?
G   Who directed *My Man Godfrey ('36)*?
H   When did she become **Mrs Clark Gable**?
I   Who portrayed her husband in *Mr and Mrs Smith ('41)*?
J   What was the title of her last movie?

P1202·41

23 Child's Play: Young Performers of the Screen
Specialist; worth 4 points each

A Who portrayed the children terrorised by **Robert Mitchum** in *The Night of the Hunter ('55)*?

B Where and when was **Shirley Temple** born?

C Who gained the nickname **Moochie**?

D Name **Brandon de Wilde's** début movie.

E Who portrayed **Hayley Mills'**

brother and sister in *Whistle Down the Wind ('62)*?

F Which child actor appeared in *The Grapes of Wrath ('40)*, *Keeper of the Flame ('42)* and *Rhapsody in Blue ('45)*?

G In which long-running TV series did **Tommy Rettig** portray the character **Jeff**?

H Who portrayed **Wallace Beery's** son in *The Champ ('31)*?

I Name the 1950 movie in which **Gigi Perreau** portrayed **Natalie Wood's** sister?

J By which name was **Sandra Lee Henville** better known?

K Who portrayed **Henry Spofford III** in *Gentlemen Prefer Blondes ('53)*?

L What colour hair did **Dean Stockwell** once sport?

M Who portrayed **Boy** in *Tarzan Finds A Son ('39)*, *Tarzan's Secret Treasure ('41)*, *Tarzan's New York Adventure ('42)*, *Tarzan Triumphs ('43)*, *Tarzan's Desert Mystery ('43)*, *Tarzan and the Amazons ('45)* and *Tarzan and the Leopard Woman ('46)*?

N In which 1958 western did **David Ladd** appear opposite his father **Alan Ladd**?

O Which year saw the release of **Disney's** *Swiss Family Robinson*?

P Name the character **Kevin Corcoran** portrayed in *Pollyana ('60)*.

Q What was the name of **Ted Donaldson's** pet caterpillar in *Once Upon a Time ('44)*?

R Who in 1953 did **Brandon de Wilde** ask to come back?

S Who portrayed **Michael Darling** in *Peter Pan ('25)*?

T Name **Kevin Corcoran's** actress sister.

U Who earned the nickname **Pudge**?

V He portrayed **Dan Dailey's** son in *The Kid from Left Field ('53)*, **Richard Todd's** in *A Man Called Peter ('54)* and **Victor Mature's** in *Violent Saturday ('55)*. Who is he?

W In which movie was **Natalie Wood** rescued by **Orson Welles**?

X Who portrayed **Toby Nearly** in *Close Encounters of the Third Kind ('77)*?

Y Under which category did **Tatum O'Neal** receive her Oscar for *Paper Moon ('73)*?

Z **Tallulah, Doodle, Lizzy, Dandy Dan, Blousey** and **Cagey Joe** were all characters in which movie?

Tarzan's Secret Treasure (see 23 M)

Mystery Star 6
Clues are set on a diminishing points' scale with (a) worth 5 and (e) worth 1.

A Male, born Pickway, Kansas, October 4 1892.

B Christened **Joseph Francis**.

C At the age of three he joined his parents' vaudeville act.

D Appeared in many two-reelers with **Roscoe 'Fatty' Arbuckle**.

E His movies include: *The General ('26)*, *Hollywood Cavalcade ('39)*, *Limelight ('52)* and *How to Stuff a Wild Bikini ('65)*.

24 The Movie Makers: Alfred Hitchcock

Specialist; worth 4 points each

A   Name his début movie.
B   When did he leave England for Hollywood?

C   He directed Britain's first talkie; what was its title?
D   Who was his assistant director on *Psycho ('60)?*
E   What was the title of the last movie he made in England?

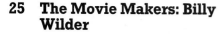

25 The Movie Makers: Billy Wilder

Specialist; worth 4 points each

A   Where and when was he born?
B   What was his original profession?
C   Name his début movie as a director.
D   Who was his screenwriting partner for such movies as *Ninotchka ('39), The Lost Weekend ('45)* and *Hold Back The Dawn ('41)?*
E   How many Oscars did he receive for *The Apartment ('60)* and name the categories?

Star Couple 2
General; worth 2 points each

Identify this 'on and off' screen couple.

Film Poster 3
General; worth 2 points each

Give the title of the film this poster is advertising.

26 The Players: John Wayne
Specialist; worth 4 points each

A Where and when was he born?
B What was his real name?
C Who signed him for *The Big Trail* ('30)?
D In which movie did he portray a Scandinavian sailor?
E Who did he marry in January 1946?
F Where was *The Quiet Man* ('52) set?
G Name the 1960 movie which he produced, directed and starred in.
H Name the role and title of the movie for which he received the Academy Award for Best Actor?
I What was the title of his last movie?
J Name the characters he portrayed in:
1 *Red River* ('48)
2 *She Wore a Yellow Ribbon* ('49)
3 *Rio Grande* ('50)
4 *The Searchers* ('56)
5 *Rio Bravo* ('59)

27 Western Round-up
Specialist; worth 4 points each

A   Who portrayed **Wyatt Earp** in?
1 *Frontier Marshal ('39)*
2 *My Darling Clementine ('46)*
3 *Gunfight at the OK Corral ('57)*
4 *Hour of the Gun ('67)*
5 *Doc ('70)*

B   Who portrayed **Wild Bill Hickok** in?
1 *The Plainsman ('37)*
2 *Wild Bill Hickok Rides ('42)*
3 *Dallas ('51)*
4 *Pony Express ('53)*
5 *Calamity Jane ('53)*

C   In *The Lone Ranger ('56)* who portrayed?
1 **The Lone Ranger**
2 **Tonto**
3 **Peter Ramirez**
4 **Angry Horse**
5 **Kilgore**

D   Who directed *The Big Country ('58)*?

E   Which movie featured **Robert Wagner** and **Jeffrey Hunter** as brothers?

F   Name the actors who portrayed the **Magnificent Seven**.

G   Which character did **Eli Wallach** portray in *The Magnificent Seven ('60)*?

H   Who composed the music scores for?
1 *The Magnificent Seven ('60)*
2 *The Way West ('67)*
3 *A Fistful of Dollars ('64)*
4 *The Big Country ('58)*
5 *Hour of the Gun ('67)*

I   Which true massacre was depicted in *Soldier Blue ('70)*?

J   Who wrote the screenplay for *Jeremiah Johnson ('72)*?

K   Who narrated *Mackenna's Gold ('69)*?

L   **Tom Mix** rode five screen horses all with the same name; what was it?

M   Name the western which featured **Glenn Ford, Shirley Maclaine** and **Mickey Shaughnessy.**

N   Who portrayed **Frank Harris** in *Cowboy ('57)*?

O   Who portrayed **Stumpy** in *Rio Bravo ('59)*?

P   Name the two stars of the popular TV series *Dallas* who were seen in *The Life and Times of Judge Roy Bean ('72).*

Q   In *The Alamo ('60)* who portrayed?
1 **Sam Housten**
2 **Col William Barrett Travis**
3 **Col James Bowie**
4 **Col David Crockett**
5 **Capt. Dickerson**

R   Who directed *The Unforgiven ('60)*?

S   Who killed **John Saxon** in *The Plunderers ('60)*?

T   Who portrayed **Liberty Valance** in *The Man Who Shot Liberty Valance ('62)*?

U   Which year saw the release of the classic **Kirk Douglas** contemporary western *Lonely Are The Brave?*

V   Which movie featured the character **Preacher Quint**?

W   Who directed *The Good The Bad and The Ugly ('67)*?

X   Which western featured singer **Nat King Cole**?

Y   Name the **Disney** movie in which **Robert Loggia** portrayed a Mexican lawman.

Z   Who directed the 1943 **Jane Russell** movie *The Outlaw?*

Jeremiah Johnson
(see 27 J)

28 The Movie Makers: James Stewart
Specialist; worth 4 points each

A   Where and when was he born?

B   What is his full name?

C   Name his début movie and the character he portrayed.

D   In which movie did he portray **Macaulay Connor**?

E   Which character did he portray in?
1 *The Stratton Story ('49)*
2 *Harvey ('50)*
3 *The Spirit of St Louis ('57)*
4 *Night Passage ('57)*
5 *Cheyenne Autumn ('64)*

29 The Movie Makers: Robert Mitchum
Specialist; worth 4 points each

A   Where and when was he born?

B   Name his début movie.

C   With which song (from a film) did he make the pop music charts?

D   Where was *The Sundowners ('60)* set?

E   Who directed *Ryan's Daughter ('71)*?

Robert Mitchum
(see 29)

30 The Players: Kirk Douglas
Specialist; worth 4 points each

A   Where and when was he born?
B   By which name was he originally known?
C   Name his début movie.
D   Who directed *Champion ('49)*?
E   What is the alternative title for *Ace In the Hole ('51)*?
F   For which 1952 movie was he nominated for an Academy Award as Best Actor?
G   Name his 1954 **Walt Disney** movie.
H   What was the title of the song he sang in *The Last Sunset ('61)*?
I   Name the movie in which he co-starred with singer **Johnny Cash.**
J   In which movies did he portray these characters?
   1 **Vincent Van Gogh**
   2 **Mickey Marcus**
   3 **Doc Holliday**
   4 **Colonel Dax**
   5 **Brendan O'Malley**

31 The Movie Makers: Errol Flynn
Specialist; worth 4 points each

A Where was he born?
B What was his full name?
C Name his début movie.
D In which movie did he portray the actor **John Barrymore**?
E Just before his death in 1959 he completed his second autobiographical book *My Wicked Wicked Ways* ; what was the title of the first?

32 The Movie Makers: Orson Welles
Specialist; worth 4 points each

A Where and when was he born?
B When did he broadcast the controversial radio play *Invasion From Mars* (full date)?
C Name his début movie as a director.
D Which character did he portray in *The Third Man* ('49)?
E In 1970 he won a special Oscar for supreme artistry and versatility in the creation of motion pictures. Under which category did he win his first Academy Award in 1941?

33 Screen Test
General; worth 2 points each

A What was **Glenda Jackson's** occupation in *A Touch of Class* ('72)?
B What was **George Segal's** occupation in *Loving* ('70)?
C Who narrated *John F. Kennedy:*
Years of Lightning, Day of Drums ('64)?
D Who was the first screen actor to become the President of the United States and when (full date)?
E Name the 1976 movie in which both **Paul Newman** and **Harold Gould** appeared.
F In *My Fair Lady* ('64) who portrayed?
1 **Eliza**
2 **Professor Higgins**
3 **Alfred Doolittle**
4 **Colonel Pickering**
5 **Mrs Higgins**
G By which name was **Bob Hope** originally known?
H Who portrayed **Phileas Fogg** in *Around The World in Eighty Days* ('56)?
I Name **Tatum O'Neal's** début movie.
J Which character did **Ryan O'Neal** portray in the TV soap opera *Peyton Place*?
K Which actor was once known as **James Stewart**?
L Who portrayed **Stanley X** in *Wild in the Streets* ('68)?
M Where was **Anthony Quinn** born?
N Who directed *Shadows* ('59)?
O Name **Dorothy Harrington's** actress daughter.
P Who composed the music scores for?
1 *Breakfast At Tiffanys* ('61)
2 *Charade* ('63)
3 *Days of Wine and Roses* ('62)
4 *The Way We Were* ('73)
5 *Two for the Road* ('67)
Q Name the first movie which had a musical score and sound effects linked directly to the screen action.
R Name **Lee Grant's** début movie.
S What has Academy Award winner **Edith Head** contributed to many movies?
T What was **Hy Hazell's** full name?
U When was *The Cruel Sea* released?
V Which 1937 movie featured the fictional Tibetan Utopia Shangri-La?
W Who was **Nelson Eddy's** leading lady in a string of film operettas?
X Which musical included such song classics as 'The Trolley Song', 'Have Yourself A Merry Little Christmas' and 'You and I'?
Y Name the sequel to the 1959 movie *Room at the Top*.
Z Who conceived the idea of the notorious girls' school St Trinian's?

Glenda Jackson
(see 33 A)

The Way We Were
(see 33 P)

Orson Welles (see 32)

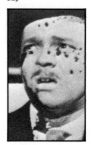

The Big Picture Quiz 6:
From Here to Eternity
Specialist; worth 4 points each

A   Which year was it released?
B   Who directed it?
C   On whose novel was it based?
D   Who was the producer?
E   Where was the infantry barracks at
     the centre of the story?
F   Who wrote the screenplay?
G   What was **Lorene's** occupation?
H   Which battle is featured in the movie?
I   How many Oscars did the film win,
     who won them and under which
     categories?
J   Who portrayed these characters?
     1 **Robert E. Lee Prewitt**
     2 **Sgt Milton Warden**
     3 **Karen Holmes**
     4 **Angelo Maggio**
     5 **Corp. Buckley**

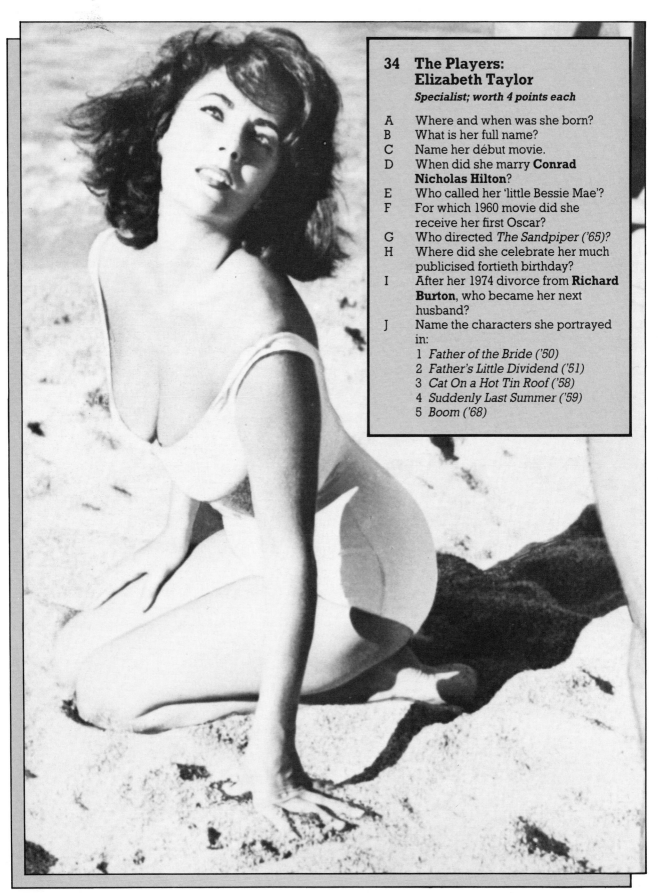

34 The Players: Elizabeth Taylor
Specialist; worth 4 points each

A   Where and when was she born?

B   What is her full name?

C   Name her début movie.

D   When did she marry **Conrad Nicholas Hilton**?

E   Who called her 'little Bessie Mae'?

F   For which 1960 movie did she receive her first Oscar?

G   Who directed *The Sandpiper* ('65)?

H   Where did she celebrate her much publicised fortieth birthday?

I   After her 1974 divorce from **Richard Burton**, who became her next husband?

J   Name the characters she portrayed in:

     1   *Father of the Bride* ('50)

     2   *Father's Little Dividend* ('51)

     3   *Cat On a Hot Tin Roof* ('58)

     4   *Suddenly Last Summer* ('59)

     5   *Boom* ('68)

Mystery star 7

Clues are set on a diminishing points scale with (a) worth 5 and (e) worth 1.

A   Female, born St Joseph, Mo. January 4 1914.
B   Christened **Sara Jane Faulks**.
C   One time wife of **Ronald Reagan**.
D   Won Academy Award for Best Actress in 1948.
E   Her movies include: *The Lost Weekend ('45), Magnificent Obsession ('54), Pollyanna ('60)* and *How to Commit Marriage ('69).*

35   The Movie Makers: Cary Grant

Specialist; worth 4 points each

A   Where was he born?
B   By which name was he originally known?
C   Name his début film.
D   In which movie did he portray composer **Cole Porter**?
E   When did he receive his special Oscar for his unique mastery of the art of screen acting?

36   The Movie Makers: Rudy Vallee

Specialist; worth 4 points each

A   Where and when was he born?
B   What is his full name?
C   Name his début movie.
D   Which character did he portray in *Gold Diggers In Paris ('38)?*
E   He made a comeback in the sixties with a highly successful Broadway musical and movie; what was its title?

37   The Movie Makers: Dirk Bogarde

Specialist; worth 4 points each

A   What is his full name?
B   Name his début movie and the character he portrayed?
C   What was his occupation in *Victim ('61)?*
D   In which movie did he co-star with **Judy Garland**?
E   Name the movies in which he portrayed:
    1 **Bill Fox**
    2 **Tom Riley**
    3 **Franz Liszt**
    4 **George Hathaway**
    5 **Simon Sparrow**

Star Couple 3
General; worth 2 points each

Identify this 'on and off' screen couple.

38 The Songs
General; worth 2 points each

Which films do you associate with these songs?
A   The Windmills of Your Mind
B   All The Way
C   Lullaby of Broadway
D   We May Never Love Like This Again
E   Moon River
F   The Way You Look Tonight
G   Raindrops Keep Fallin' On My Head
H   The Continental
I   On The Atchison, Topeka and Santa Fe
J   For All We Know
K   Secret Love
L   It Might As Well Be Spring
M   The Shadow of Your Smile
N   You'll Never Know
O   Evergreen
P   Mona Lisa
Q   Lady Be Good
R   I'm Easy
S   Zip-A-Dee-Doo-Dah
T   High Hopes
U   White Christmas
V   Que Sera, Sera
W   Call Me Irresponsible
X   Baby It's Cold Outside
Y   In the Cool, Cool, Cool of the Evening
Z   When You Wish Upon A Star

Gregory Peck (see 39)

39 The Movie Makers: Gregory Peck
Specialist; worth 4 points each

A   Where and when was he born?
B   What is his full name?
C   Name his début movie.
D   For which role did he receive the Academy Award for Best Actor in 1963?
E   What was his involvement with *The Dove* ('74)?

◼️◼️◼️◼️◼️◼️◼️

Mystery Star 8
Clues are set on a diminishing points' scale with (a) worth 5 and (e) worth 1.

A   Female, born Brooklyn, New York, August 17 1892.
B   Appeared in vaudeville at the age of fourteeen.
C   Later in burlesque as **Baby Vamp**.
D   Autobiography 1959 *Goodness Had Nothing To Do With It.*
E   Her movies include: *I'm No Angel* ('33), *Klondyke Annie* ('36), *My Little Chickadee* ('39) and *Myra Breckinridge* ('69).

40 The Players: Laurence Olivier

Specialist; worth 4 points each

A   Where and when was he born?
B   What is his full name and title?
C   Who became his first wife?
D   Name his début film.
E   In which film did he compete with **Adolphe Menjou** for the affection of **Lili Damita**?
F   Which character did he portray in *As You Like It ('36)*?
G   Who was his second wife?
H   What was the title of the first movie he directed?
I   How many Oscars did he win for *Hamlet ('48)* and under which categories?
J   In which movies did he portray these characters?
   1 **Mr Darcy**
   2 **Archie Rice**
   3 **Macheath**
   4 **Dr Spaander**
   5 **Maxim de Winter**

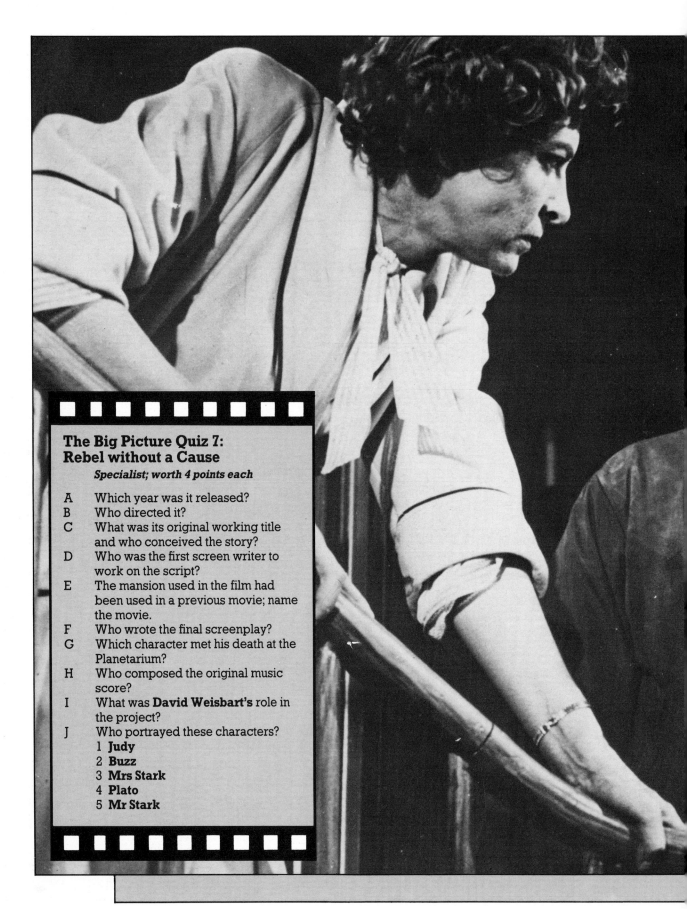

The Big Picture Quiz 7: Rebel without a Cause

Specialist; worth 4 points each

A   Which year was it released?

B   Who directed it?

C   What was its original working title and who conceived the story?

D   Who was the first screen writer to work on the script?

E   The mansion used in the film had been used in a previous movie; name the movie.

F   Who wrote the final screenplay?

G   Which character met his death at the Planetarium?

H   Who composed the original music score?

I   What was **David Weisbart's** role in the project?

J   Who portrayed these characters?
1 **Judy**
2 **Buzz**
3 **Mrs Stark**
4 **Plato**
5 **Mr Stark**

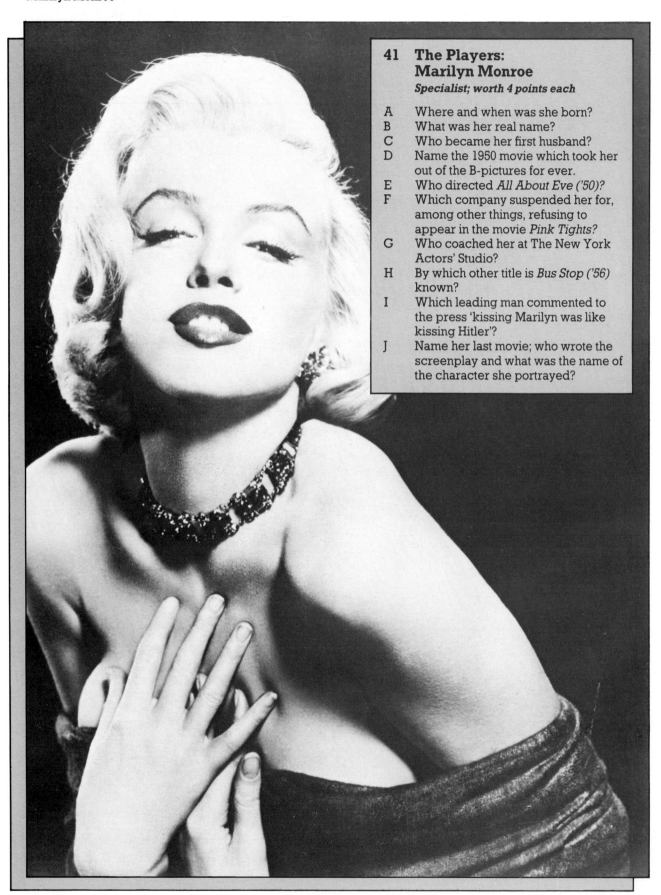

41 The Players: Marilyn Monroe
Specialist; worth 4 points each

A Where and when was she born?

B What was her real name?

C Who became her first husband?

D Name the 1950 movie which took her out of the B-pictures for ever.

E Who directed *All About Eve* ('50)?

F Which company suspended her for, among other things, refusing to appear in the movie *Pink Tights*?

G Who coached her at The New York Actors' Studio?

H By which other title is *Bus Stop* ('56) known?

I Which leading man commented to the press 'kissing Marilyn was like kissing Hitler'?

J Name her last movie; who wrote the screenplay and what was the name of the character she portrayed?

42 War Games
Specialist; worth 4 points each

A Who portrayed **Captain Walker** in *The Story of GI Joe* ('45)?

B Which year saw the release of *The Desert Fox*?

C Who directed *Sink the Bismarck* ('60)?

D Name the character **William Holden** portrayed in *Stalag 17* ('53).

E What was the title of the march used in *The Bridge on the River Kwai* ('57) and who composed it?

F Who portrayed **Franz Von Werra** in *The One That Got Away* ('55)?

G Which war was featured in *The Green Berets* ('68)?

H Name the movie in which **Gregory Peck** portrayed **Brigadier-General Frank Savage**.

I Which character did **Steve McQueen** play in *Hell is for Heroes* ('61)?

J Who portrayed **J.F. Kennedy** in *PT 109* ('63)?

K In which year was *All Quiet on the Western Front* released?

L How many Oscars did *The Bridge on the River Kwai* ('57) receive?

M Which war was featured in *The Bridges of Toko-Ri* ('55)?

N Who did **Virginia McKenna** portray in the true life story *Carve Her Name with Pride* ('57)?

O Who was reported to have retitled *Where Eagles Dare* ('69) as *Where Doubles Dare*?

P Which movie featured forty-three international stars including **Richard Beymer, Henry Fonda, Curt Jurgens, Michael Medwin** and **Irina Demich**?

Q Name the three directors of *Tora! Tora! Tora!* ('70).

R Who led **The Dirty Dozen**?

S Who composed the original music score for *633 Squadron* ('64)?

T Name the six actors who portrayed the commandos in *The Guns of Navarone* ('61).

U What was the graffiti daubed on **Major King's** nuclear warheads in **Kubrick's** *Dr Strangelove* ('63)?

V Where was *Yanks* ('80) set?

W In *Patton: Lust for Glory* ('69) who portrayed

Yanks (see 42 V)

1 **General George S. Patton**
2 **General Omar N. Bradley**

X What did the title *Ice Cold In Alex* ('60) refer to?

Y Who directed *A Farewell to Arms* ('32)?

Z Which 1970 movie was set in a mobile hospital during the Korean War?

Star Couple 4
General; worth 2 points each

Identify this 'on and off' screen couple.

The Big Picture Quiz 8:
King Creole

Specialist; worth 4 points each

A   Which year was it released?
B   Who directed it?
C   On whose novel was it based?
D   What was the title of the original
     story?
E   Who was the producer?
F   Where was the story set?
G   Who composed the title song?
H   What was **Col. Tom Parker** credited
     as?
I   Who wrote the screenplay?
J   Who portrayed these characters?
     1 **Danny Stone**
     2 **Ronnie**
     3 **Maxie Fields**
     4 **Shark**
     5 **Nellie**

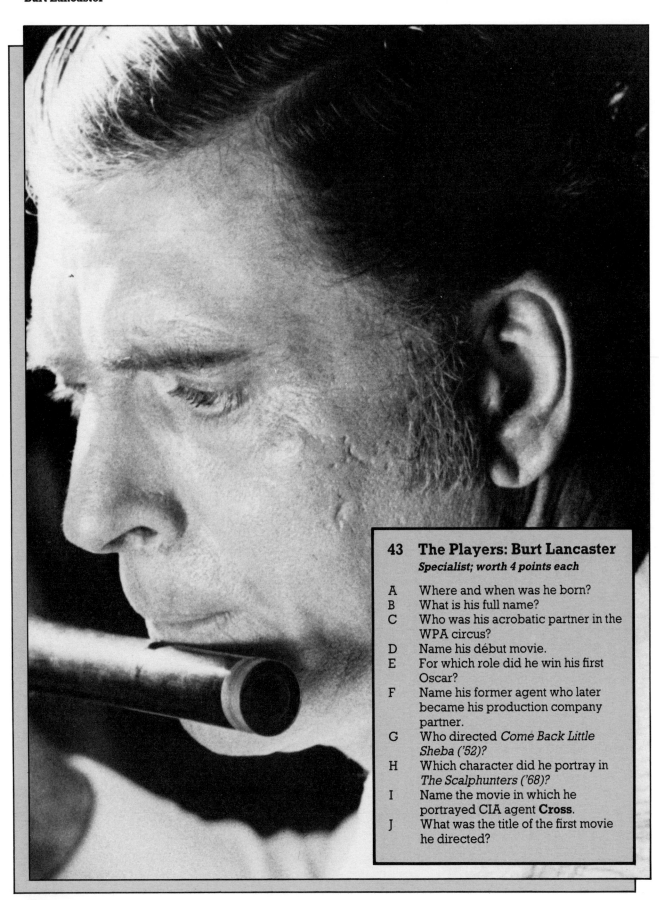

43 The Players: Burt Lancaster
Specialist; worth 4 points each

A Where and when was he born?
B What is his full name?
C Who was his acrobatic partner in the WPA circus?
D Name his début movie.
E For which role did he win his first Oscar?
F Name his former agent who later became his production company partner.
G Who directed *Come Back Little Sheba* ('52)?
H Which character did he portray in *The Scalphunters* ('68)?
I Name the movie in which he portrayed CIA agent **Cross**.
J What was the title of the first movie he directed?

44 Stage Names
Specialist; worth 3 points each

By which names are the following better known?

A   **Bernard Schwarz**
B   **Carlo Pedersoli**
C   **Reginald Truscott-Jones**
D   **Walter Palanuik**
E   **Helen Koford**
F   **Edward Breitenberger**
G   **Marjorie Robertson**
H   **Archibald Leach**
I   **Melvyn Hesselberg**
J   **Lesley Hornby**
K   **Virginia Jones**
L   **Lewis D. Offield**
M   **Blanca Rosa Welter**
N   **Louis Bert Lindley**
O   **Estelle O'Brien Thompson**
P   **Ruby Stevens**
Q   **Mario Moreno**
R   **Françoise Sorya**
S   **Dominic Felix Amici**
T   **Julia Wells**
U   **George Augustus Andrews**
V   **Francis Avallone**
W   **Anna Maria Italiano**
X   **William Berkeley Enos**
Y   **William Millar**
Z   **Patrick Cheesman**

45 Screen Test
General; worth 2 points each

A   Where was **Raquel Welch** born?
B   Which movie marked **Robert Redford's** directional début?
C   Who portrayed **Sir Love-A-Lot** in **Clint Eastwood's** *Breezy* ('73)?
D   Which year saw the release of *O Lucky Man!*?
E   Where was *The Exorcist* ('73) set?
F   Name **William Holden's** début movie.
G   In *The Glenn Miller Story* ('54) who portrayed?
     1   **Glenn Miller**
     2   **Helen Miller**
     3   **Don Haynes**
     4   **Polly Haynes**
     5   **Louis Armstrong**
H   Who wrote the original story on which *The Last American Hero* ('73) was based?
I   Which famous battle was featured in *The Last Command* ('55)?
J   Who directed *Performance* ('70)?
K   Which Olympics formed the background to *Walk Don't Run* ('66)?
L   What was **Efrem Zimbalist Jr's** profession in *Wait until Dark* ('67)?
M   Who portrayed **Pierre** in *War and Peace* ('56)?
N   Who were **Doris Day's** leading men in?
     1   *Caprice* ('67)
     2   *Please Don't Eat the Daisies* ('60)
     3   *Move Over Darling* ('63)
     4   *Pillow Talk* ('59)
     5   *That Touch of Mink* ('62)
     6   *Do Not Disturb* ('65)
O   Which character did **Bette Davis** portray in *A Pocketful of Miracles* ('61)?
P   Where was *Black Orpheus* ('59) set?
Q   Name **Diane Keaton's** first movie with **Woody Allen**.
R   Whose story was featured in *Somebody up there Likes Me* ('56)?
S   Name the composers whose stories were told in:
     1   *A Song To Remember* ('45)
     2   *The Music Lovers* ('70)
     3   *Song Without End* ('60)
     4   *The Magnificent Rebel* ('60)
     5   *Song of Norway* ('70)
T   Which 1943 movie featured the character **Count Alucard**?
U   Which actor did **Tony Curtis** impersonate in *Some Like It Hot* ('59)?
V   Which of the following films did not feature John Wayne?
     1   *Rio Bravo* ('59)
     2   *Rio Lobo* ('70)
     3   *Rio Conchos* ('64)
     4   *Rio Grande* ('56)
W   Who portrayed **James Garner's** partner in *The Skin Game* ('71)?
X   Who directed *Joe* ('70)?
Y   Which movie featured **Cliff Robertson, William Holden, Susan Strasberg, Rosalind Russell, Arthur O'Connell** and **Kim Novak** in the cast?
Z   Which battle was fought in *Zulu* ('63)?

The Last American Hero (see 45 H)

William Holden (see 45 F & Y)

Last Tango in Paris (see 46 J)

46 The Players: Marlon Brando
Specialist; worth 4 points each

A   Where and when was he born?

B   From which school was he expelled?

C   Who formed the New York Dramatic Workshop which he attended in the mid-forties?

D   Name his début movie.

E   Who directed his Oscar winning movie *On the Waterfront* ('54)?

F   In which film did he portray a Japanese interpreter?

G   Name the western he directed in 1961 and the character he played in the film.

H   Who did he portray in?
1   *Julius Caesar* ('53)
2   *The Wild One* ('53)
3   *Desirée* ('54)
4   *Mutiny on the Bounty* ('62)
5   *The Godfather* ('72)

I   His sister has appeared with him in such movies as *The Ugly American* ('65) and *The Chase* ('66). What is her name?

J   Who was his partner in *Last Tango in Paris* ('73)?

47 The Movie Makers: Brigitte Bardot

Specialist; worth 4 points each

A Who became her first husband?
B Name her début movie.
C What was the title of her first English speaking film?
D Which character did she portray in *And God Created Woman* ('56)?
E Who directed *Viva Maria* ('65)?

48 Screenplay

General; worth 2 points each

Who said the following and in which movie did they say it?

A 'I cudda been a contender. I cudda been somebody instead of a bum – which is what I am.'
B 'The prettiest sight in this fine pretty world is the sight of the privileged class enjoying its privileges.'
C 'Love means not ever having to say you're sorry.'
D 'That'll be the day.'
E 'It's injustice I hate, not Normandy.'
F 'I got vision and the rest of the world wears bifocals.'
G 'Rock 'n Roll's been going downhill ever since Buddy Holly died.'
H 'A press agent is many things, most of them punishable by law.'
I 'Special delivery. Are you expecting a beum?'
J 'The trouble with you is you're a failure to communicate.'

Star Couple 5

General; worth 2 points each

Identify this 'on and off' screen couple.

49 The Movie Makers: Tony Curtis

Specialist; worth 4 points each

A Where and when was he born?
B By which name was he originally known?
C Name his début movie.
D When did he marry **Janet Leigh**?
E Which real-life character did he portray in *The Boston Strangler* ('68)?

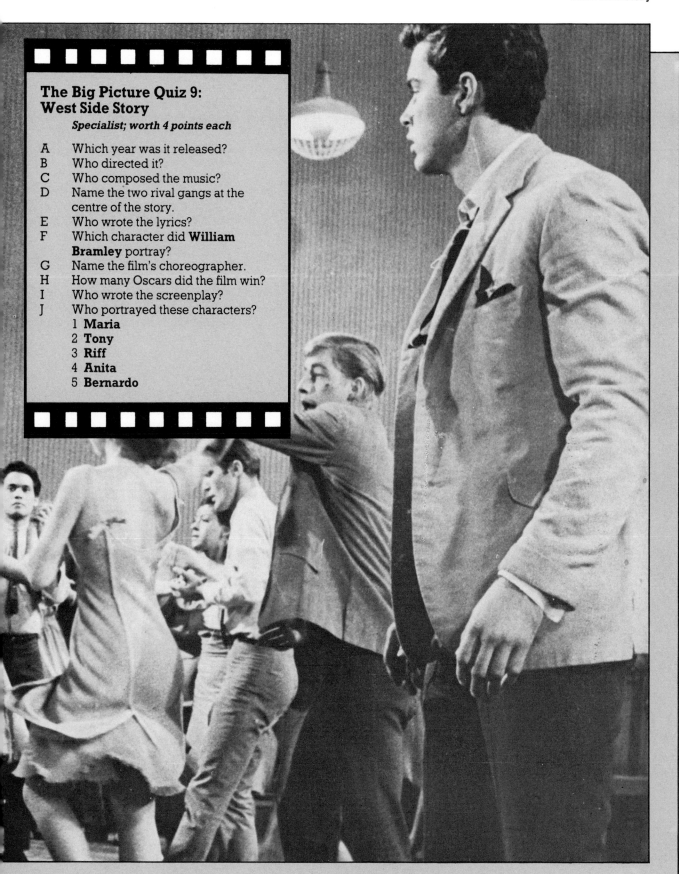

The Big Picture Quiz 9:
West Side Story

Specialist; worth 4 points each

A Which year was it released?
B Who directed it?
C Who composed the music?
D Name the two rival gangs at the centre of the story.
E Who wrote the lyrics?
F Which character did **William Bramley** portray?
G Name the film's choreographer.
H How many Oscars did the film win?
I Who wrote the screenplay?
J Who portrayed these characters?
   1 **Maria**
   2 **Tony**
   3 **Riff**
   4 **Anita**
   5 **Bernardo**

50 Screen Test
General; worth 2 points each

Mildred Pierce
(see 50 H)

A   Who portrayed **Squadron Leader Confield** in *Battle of Britain* ('69)?

B   Name the last line-up of the **Three Stooges**.

C   Where and when was **Anouk Aimée** born?

D   Who composed the music scores for?
1 *Lonely Are the Brave* ('62)
2 *Lilies of the Field* ('63)
3 *The Blue Max* ('66)

4 *Planet of the Apes* ('68)
5 *The Boys From Brazil* ('79)

E   Which 1973 movie made extensive use of **Scott Joplin's** music?

F   Name the stars of *Hell in the Pacific* ('68).

G   **Alan Arkin** was once a member of which 1950s vocal group?

H   Who directed *Mildred Pierce* ('45)?

I   What was the sub-title added to the

up-dated version of *Close Encounters of the Third Kind* ('80)?

J   Where was *Ice Palace* ('60) set?

K   Name **Richard Boone's** 1957–61 western TV series and the character he portrayed.

L   Who loved **Mozart, Bach,** the **Beatles** and **Oliver Barrett IV**?

M   Who became the third **Mrs Laurence Olivier**?

N   In *It's A Mad Mad Mad Mad World* ('63) who portrayed?
1 **Smiler Grogen**
2 **Capt. C.G. Culpeper**
3 **J. Algernon Hawthorne**
4 **Emmeline Finch**
5 **Mrs Marcus**

O   When was *Bonnie and Clyde* released?

P   Who portrayed the young lovers in *The Blue Lagoon* ('49) and *The Blue Lagoon* ('80)?

Q   Name **Charlie Ruggles'** actor brother.

R   Who directed *Elvira Madigan* ('67)?

S   Who did **Gene Hackman** portray in *A Bridge Too Far* ('78)?

T   What was **Little Nellie** in *You Only Live Twice* ('67)?

U   What has **Jean Burt Riley's** contribution been to the movie industry?

V   Who said 'When I'm good I'm very good. When I'm bad I'm better'?

W   Name the **Disney** movies in which these songs were originally featured:
1 Let's Get Together
2 I've Got No Strings
3 Bare Necessities
4 Second Star to the Right
5 The Monkey's Uncle

X   In which movie did **Kirk Douglas** portray the character **Mike Wayne**?

Y   Whose autobiography was entitled *Tall, Dark and Gruesome?*

Z   In *Goldfinger* ('54) who portrayed **Pussy Galore**?

Mystery Star 9
Clues are set on a diminishing points' scale with (a) worth 5 and (e) worth 1.

A   Male, born Hot Springs, Ark., September 3 1913.

B   Moved to California in his teens.

C   Married his agent **Sue Carrol** in 1942.

D   Was once dubbed 'Tight-lipped violence'.

E   His movies include: *Once in a Lifetime* ('32), *Citizen Kane* ('41), *Shane* ('53) and *Guns of the Timberland* ('60).

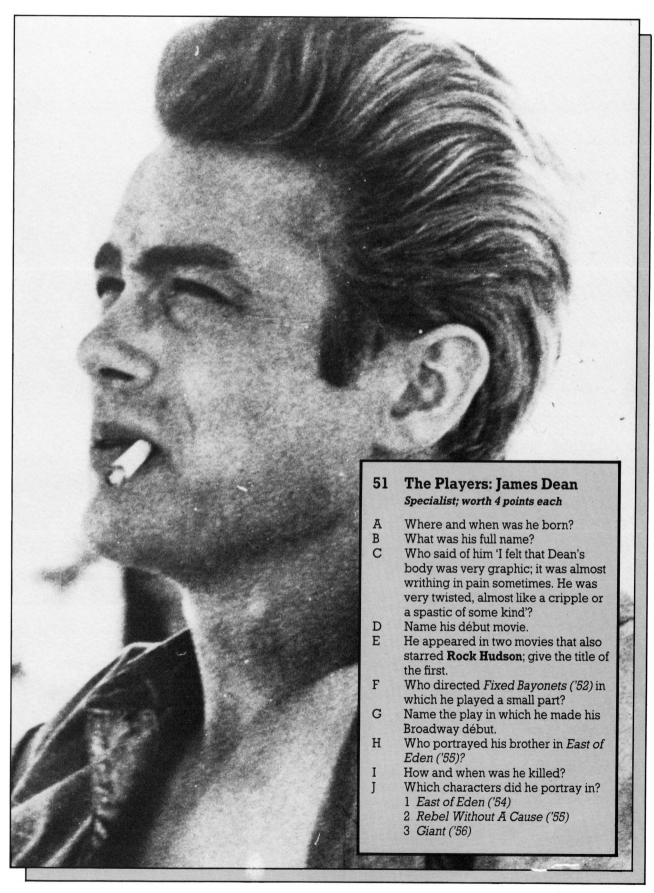

51 The Players: James Dean
Specialist; worth 4 points each

A   Where and when was he born?

B   What was his full name?

C   Who said of him 'I felt that Dean's body was very graphic; it was almost writhing in pain sometimes. He was very twisted, almost like a cripple or a spastic of some kind'?

D   Name his début movie.

E   He appeared in two movies that also starred **Rock Hudson**; give the title of the first.

F   Who directed *Fixed Bayonets* ('52) in which he played a small part?

G   Name the play in which he made his Broadway début.

H   Who portrayed his brother in *East of Eden* ('55)?

I   How and when was he killed?

J   Which characters did he portray in?
    1 *East of Eden* ('54)
    2 *Rebel Without A Cause* ('55)
    3 *Giant* ('56)

Star Couple 6
General; worth 2 points each

Identify this 'on and off' screen couple.

52 The Movie Makers: Sophia Loren
Specialist; worth 4 points each

A By which name was she originally known?
B Name her début movie.
C What was the title of her first movie with **Marcello Mastroianni**?
D Who did she marry in September 1957?
E Which 1961 movie won her the Oscar for Best Actress?

53 The Movie Makers: Jack Lemmon
Specialist; worth 4 points each

A Where and when was he born?
B What is his full name?
C Name his début movie.
D In which movie did he portray **Joe Clay**?
E He won an Oscar in 1955 for Best Supporting Actor and another in 1973 for Best Actor. Name the movies and the characters he portrayed.

54 The Movie Makers: Peter Finch
Specialist; worth 4 points each

A Where and when was he born?
B By which name was he originally known?
C Name his début movie.
D Which character did he portray in **Disney's** *Robin Hood ('51)*?
E Name the movies in which he portrayed these characters:
1 **Dr Daniel Hirsh**
2 **Flambeau**
3 **Langsdorff**
4 **Oscar Wilde**
5 **Howard Beale**

55 The Players: Elvis Presley
Specialist; worth 4 points each

A   Where and when was he born?

B   What was his full name?

C   Name his début movie.

D   Who directed *Jailhouse Rock ('57)?*

E   Name the first movie he made after his discharge from the American Army.

F   Who was originally sought for **Elvis'** role in *Flaming Star ('60)?*

G   He appeared in a movie co-starring **Charles Bronson**. What was its title?

H   Name the movie in which **Ursula Andress** was his leading lady.

I   Who directed *Elvis – that's the Way It Is ('70)?*

J   Name the movies in which he portrayed these characters:
  1 **Dr John Carpenter**
  2 **Joe Lightcloud**
  3 **Jess Wade**
  4 **Deke Rivers**
  5 **Charlie Rogers**

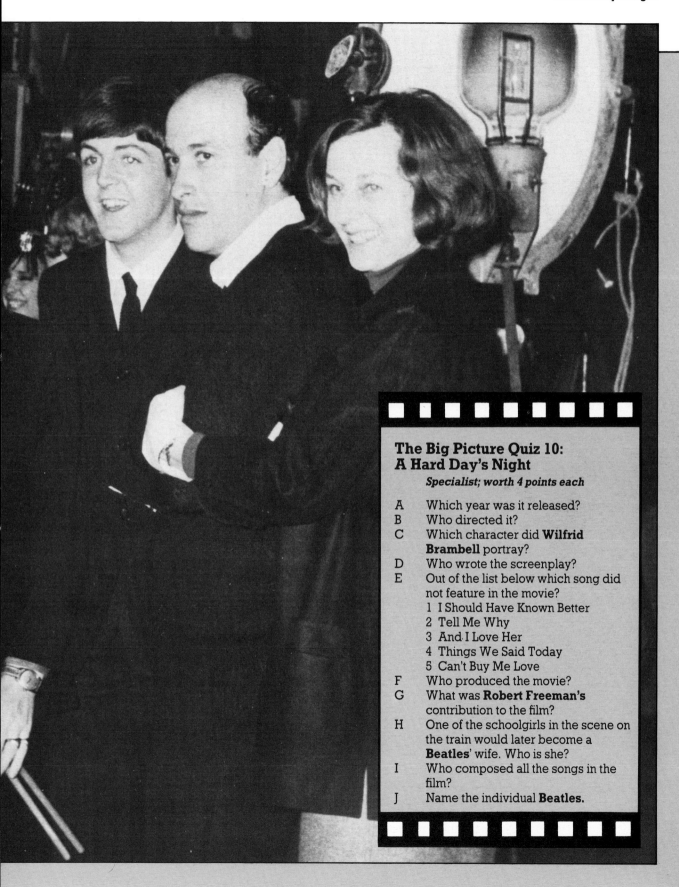

**The Big Picture Quiz 10:
A Hard Day's Night**
Specialist; worth 4 points each

A   Which year was it released?
B   Who directed it?
C   Which character did **Wilfrid Brambell** portray?
D   Who wrote the screenplay?
E   Out of the list below which song did not feature in the movie?
      1 I Should Have Known Better
      2 Tell Me Why
      3 And I Love Her
      4 Things We Said Today
      5 Can't Buy Me Love
F   Who produced the movie?
G   What was **Robert Freeman's** contribution to the film?
H   One of the schoolgirls in the scene on the train would later become a **Beatles'** wife. Who is she?
I   Who composed all the songs in the film?
J   Name the individual **Beatles**.

Mystery Star 10

Clues are set on a diminishing points' scale with (a) worth 5 and (e) worth 1.

A   Male, born London, September 17 1928.
B   Made his screen début at the age of eight.
C   Moved to Hollywood, signed with Twentieth Century-Fox in 1941.
D   Also gained reputation as a photographer.
E   His movies include: *Murder In the Family ('36)*, *Thunderhead ('45)*, *The Subterraneans ('60)* and *The Poseidon Adventure ('72)*.

---

56   The Movie Makers: Sidney Poitier

Specialist; worth 4 points each

A   Where was he born?
B   Name his début movie.
C   In which movie did he portray the character **Gregory W. Miller**?
D   Name the three movies in which he played **Virgil Tibbs**.
E   What was the title of the first movie he directed?

57   The Movie Makers: James Garner

Specialist; worth 4 points each

A   By which name was he originally known?
B   Name his début movie.
C   In which movie did he portray **Wyatt Earp**?
D   Who directed both *Support Your Local Sheriff ('69)* and *Support Your Local Gunfighter ('71)*?
E   Name the three TV series he made between 1957 and 1978.

Mystery Star 11

Clues are set on a diminishing points' scale with (a) worth 5 and (e) worth 1.

A   Female, born Beverly Hills, Calif., May 9 1946.
B   Daughter of a ventriloquist and character actor.
C   Once remarked 'I may not be a great actress, but I've become the greatest at screen orgasms...ten seconds of heavy breathing, roll your head from side to side, simulate a slight asthma attack and die a little!'
D   Also acknowledged as a photo-journalist and dramatist.
E   Her movies include: *The Sand Pebbles ('66)*, *Vivre Pour Vivre ('67)*, *Getting Straight ('70)* and *The Hunting Party ('71)*.

58 The Players:
Audrey Hepburn
Specialist; worth 4 points each

A Where and when was she born?

B What is her full name?

C Name her début movie.

D Who did she marry on September 25 1954?

E Which movie won her the Oscar for Best Actress?

F Name the movie in which she appeared opposite **Humphrey Bogart**.

G Which character did she portray in *War and Peace* ('56)?

H Who directed *The Nun's Story* ('59)?

I In which movie did she portray the character **Holly Golightly**?

J Who was her leading man in *Two For The Road* ('66)?

59 Screen Test
General; worth 2 points each

A In *Cabaret* ('72) who portrayed **Emcee**?

B Who directed *I Am a Fugitive from a Chain Gang* ('32)?

C Name the **Mel Brooks'** movies in which the songs below were featured:
1 Hope for the Best, Expect the Worst
2 I'm Tired
3 Puttin' on the Ritz
4 If You Love Me Baby, Tell Me Loud
5 Springtime for Hitler

D Who portrayed **Gable** and **Lombard** in the film of the same name?

E Which movie featured **Erich von Stroheim** as **Field Marshal Rommel**?

F Name **Jane Fonda's** début movie.

G Which character did **Henry Fonda** portray in the TV western series *The Deputy* ('59–'60)?

H By which name was **Leland T. Weed** better known?

I Name the movie in which **Paul Newman** and **Steve McQueen** co-starred.

J Which character did **Dean Martin** portray in *The Silencers* ('66), *Murderer's Row* ('66), *The Ambushers* ('67) and *Wrecking Crew* ('69)?

Richard Burton (see 59 W)

Dean Martin (see 59 J)

K Name the sports personalities portrayed by:
1 **Ronald Reagan** in *The Winning Team* ('52)
2 **Gary Cooper** in *The Pride of the Yankees* ('42)
3 **Anthony Perkins** in *Fear Strikes Out* ('57)
4 **Glenn Ford** in *Follow the Sun* ('51)
5 **Esther Williams** in *Million Dollar Mermaid* ('52)

L Who narrated *Those Magnificent Men in Their Flying Machines* ('65)?

M Who composed the music scores for *Zorba the Greek* ('65) and *Z* ('69)?

N What have **John Barrymore, Carlyle Blackwell, Arthur Wontner, Raymond Massey, Reginald Owen, Basil Rathbone, Peter Cushing, Robert Stephens** and **Peter Cook** in common?

O Which substance did **Fred McMurray** invent in *The Absent-Minded Professor* ('61)?

P When was Metro-Goldwyn-Mayer formed?

Q By which name was **John Hoeffer** better known?

R In *Tom Jones* ('63) who portrayed?
1 **Sophie Western**
2 **Squire Western**
3 **Miss Western**
4 **Lady Bellaston**
5 **Tom Jones**

S By which name was **Busby Berkeley** originally known?

T What was the surname of the family portrayed by **Frederic March, Myrna Loy, Teresa Wright** and **Michael Hall** in *The Best Years of Our Lives* ('46)?

U Name two out of the three movies that **Hywel Bennett** and **Hayley Mills** made together between 1966 and 1972.

V What was the title of **Paul le Mat's** 1975 auto movie?

W In which **Woody Allen** scripted movie did **Richard Burton** make a cameo appearance?

X Name one of the infamous **Hollywood Ten** (the group of writers, producers and directors persecuted under the 1940s **McCarthy** regime).

Y Who directed *The World of Suzie Wong* ('60)?

Z What was **Cliff Richard's** destination in *Summer Holiday* ('62)?

Star Couple 7
General; worth 2 points each

Identify this 'on and off' screen couple.

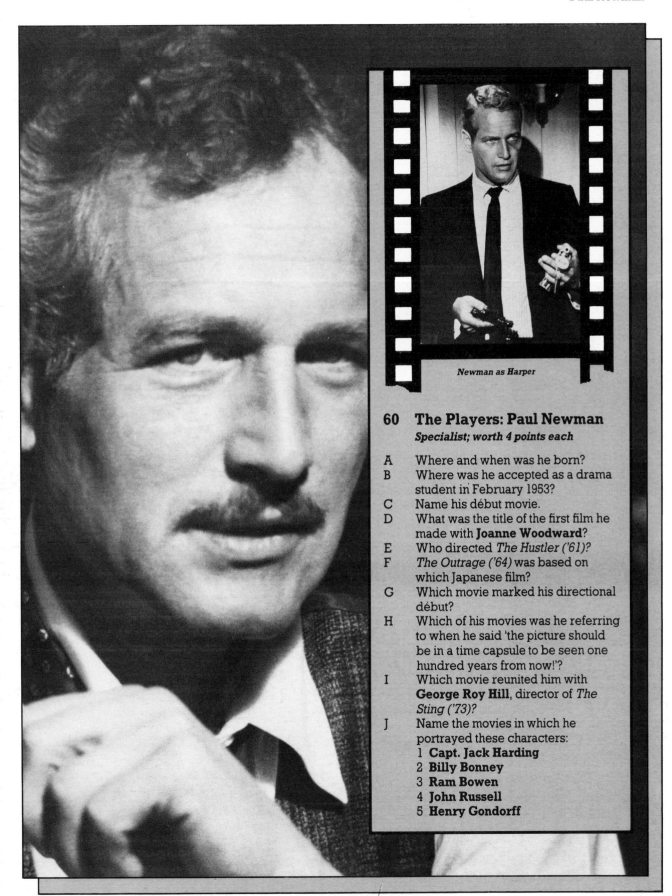

Newman as Harper

60 The Players: Paul Newman
Specialist; worth 4 points each

A   Where and when was he born?

B   Where was he accepted as a drama student in February 1953?

C   Name his début movie.

D   What was the title of the first film he made with **Joanne Woodward**?

E   Who directed *The Hustler ('61)*?

F   *The Outrage ('64)* was based on which Japanese film?

G   Which movie marked his directional début?

H   Which of his movies was he referring to when he said 'the picture should be in a time capsule to be seen one hundred years from now!'?

I   Which movie reunited him with **George Roy Hill**, director of *The Sting ('73)*?

J   Name the movies in which he portrayed these characters:
   1 **Capt. Jack Harding**
   2 **Billy Bonney**
   3 **Ram Bowen**
   4 **John Russell**
   5 **Henry Gondorff**

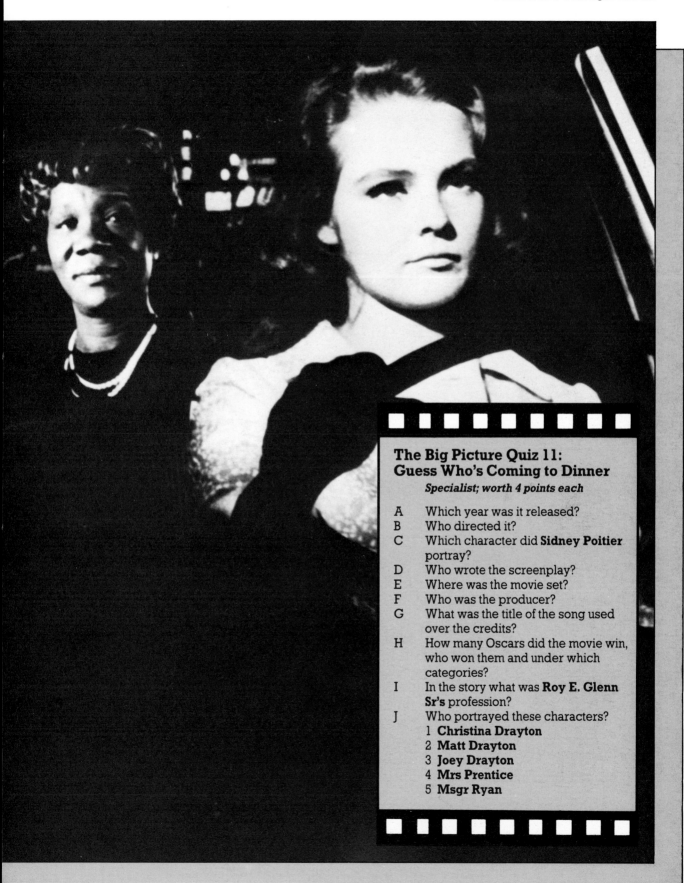

The Big Picture Quiz 11:
Guess Who's Coming to Dinner
Specialist; worth 4 points each

A   Which year was it released?
B   Who directed it?
C   Which character did **Sidney Poitier** portray?
D   Who wrote the screenplay?
E   Where was the movie set?
F   Who was the producer?
G   What was the title of the song used over the credits?
H   How many Oscars did the movie win, who won them and under which categories?
I   In the story what was **Roy E. Glenn Sr's** profession?
J   Who portrayed these characters?
     1 **Christina Drayton**
     2 **Matt Drayton**
     3 **Joey Drayton**
     4 **Mrs Prentice**
     5 **Msgr Ryan**

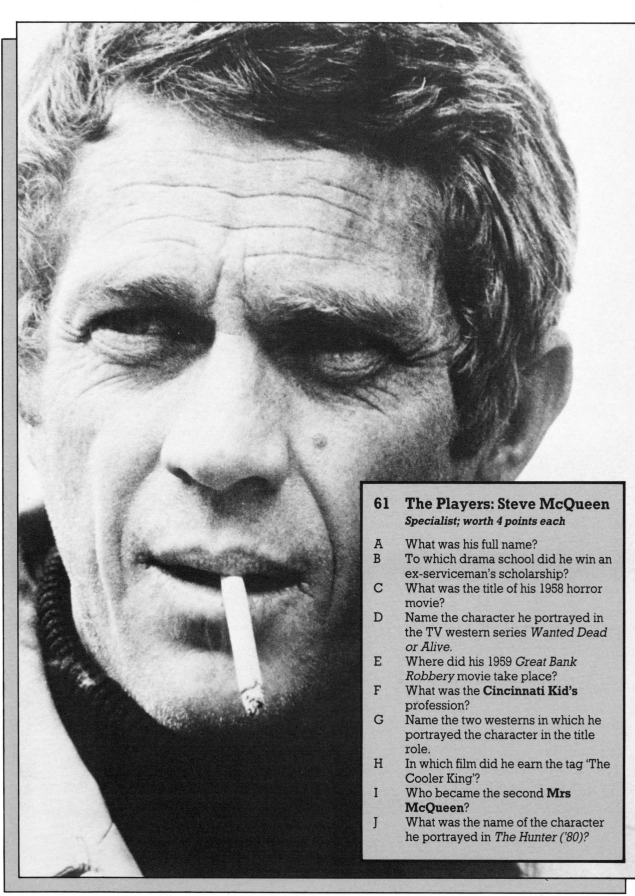

61 The Players: Steve McQueen
Specialist; worth 4 points each

A   What was his full name?

B   To which drama school did he win an ex-serviceman's scholarship?

C   What was the title of his 1958 horror movie?

D   Name the character he portrayed in the TV western series *Wanted Dead or Alive*.

E   Where did his 1959 *Great Bank Robbery* movie take place?

F   What was the **Cincinnati Kid's** profession?

G   Name the two westerns in which he portrayed the character in the title role.

H   In which film did he earn the tag 'The Cooler King'?

I   Who became the second **Mrs McQueen**?

J   What was the name of the character he portrayed in *The Hunter* ('80)?

62 The Movie Makers: Charles Bronson
Specialist; worth 4 points each

A By which name was he originally known?

B Who said of him 'He has the strongest face in the business. He is also one of its best actors'?

C Name his late fifties TV series.

D In which movies did he portray these characters?
1 **Lew Nyack**
2 **Bernado O'Reilly**
3 **J.J. Nichols**

E Who directed *The Mechanic ('72)*, *Chato's Land ('72)* and *Death Wish ('74)*?

63 The Movie Makers: James Coburn
Specialist; worth 4 points each

A Name his début movie.

B Which character did he portray in the TV series *Klondike*?

C Name the two movies in which he portrayed the secret agent **Flint**.

D With which popular TV detective series did he make his début as a director?

E Who wrote the script for his movie *The Last of Sheila ('73)*?

64 The Movie Makers: Michael Caine
Specialist; worth 4 points each

A Where and when was he born?

B By which name was he originally known?

C Name his début movie.

D Which fellow actor shared a London flat with him in the early sixties?

E Which character did he portray in *The Ipcress File ('65)*, *Funeral In Berlin ('66)* and *Billion Dollar Brain ('67)*?

Charles Bronson
(see 62)

65 The Movie Makers: Peter O'Toole
Specialist; worth 4 points each

Michael Caine
(see 64)

A Where and when was he born?

B What is his full name?

C Name his début film.

D Which character did he portray in *Beckett ('64)*?

E In which film did he play the Feature Editor of the fictitious *Chic* magazine?

66 The Movie Makers: Sean Connery
Specialist; worth 4 points each

A Where and when was he born?

B By which name was he originally known?

C Name his début movie.

D What was the title of the film in which he first portrayed the secret agent **007 James Bond**?

E Name the character he portrayed in *Zardoz ('74)*.

Sean Connery (see 66)

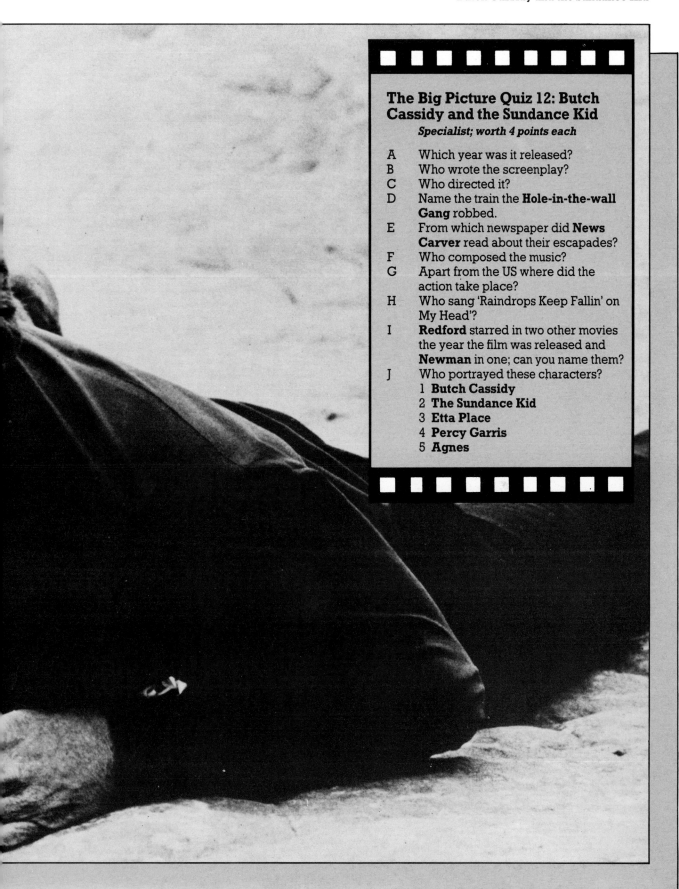

The Big Picture Quiz 12: Butch Cassidy and the Sundance Kid
Specialist; worth 4 points each

A   Which year was it released?
B   Who wrote the screenplay?
C   Who directed it?
D   Name the train the **Hole-in-the-wall Gang** robbed.
E   From which newspaper did **News Carver** read about their escapades?
F   Who composed the music?
G   Apart from the US where did the action take place?
H   Who sang 'Raindrops Keep Fallin' on My Head'?
I   **Redford** starred in two other movies the year the film was released and **Newman** in one; can you name them?
J   Who portrayed these characters?
   1 **Butch Cassidy**
   2 **The Sundance Kid**
   3 **Etta Place**
   4 **Percy Garris**
   5 **Agnes**

67 Screen Test
General; worth 2 points each

Walter Matthau (see 67 A)

A **Walter Matthau** appeared in a 1974 disaster movie under his original name; what was the name and which movie was it?

B What was the time span in *High Noon* ('52)?

C Who created the make-up for *Planet of the Apes* ('68)?

D What has **Saul Bass** contributed to movies?

E Which movie sadly marked **Edward Everett Horton's** last screen appearance?

F Who composed the music score for *The Family Way* ('66)?

G Who portrayed?
1 **George Frederick Handel** in *The Great Mr Handel* ('42)
2 **Frederic Chopin** in *Song Without End* ('60)
3 **W.C. Handy** in *St Louis Blues* ('57)
4 **Jerome Kern** in *Till the Clouds Roll By* ('47)
5 **George Gershwin** in *Rhapsody in Blue* ('45)

Popeye (see 67 N)

H Which sport is featured in *Bobby Deerfield* ('77), *Winning* ('69), *The Killers* ('64) and *A Man and A Woman* ('66)?

I Which instrumentalist and instrument were put to great use in *The Third Man* ('49)?

J Who composed the music scores for?
1 *Citizen Kane* ('41)
2 *The Magnificent Ambersons* ('42)
3 *The Trouble with Harry* ('56)
4 *North by Northwest* ('59)
5 *Psycho* ('60)

K By which name was **Lawrence Johnson** better known?

L Name **Cliff Robertson's** début movie.

M Who directed *Saturday Night and Sunday Morning* ('60)?

N Who created **Popeye** the sailorman?

O *The Magic Box* ('51) was the bio-pic of which pioneer film maker?

P Which member of the **Star Trek** crew played the lead in *Fear in the Night* ('47)?

Q Who portrayed himself in *To Hell and Back* ('55)?

R What is the title of **Anthony Quinn's** 1973 autobiography?

S How much did *Birth of A Nation* ('15) cost to make, $108,000, $110,000 or $120,000?

T Who directed?
1 *For those in Peril* ('43)
2 *Tales of Manhatten* ('42)
3 *Gaslight* ('40)
4 *Ivan* ('33)
5 *Romeo and Juliet* ('36)

U Who said of her career 'I was a junior Doris Day for years'?

V Which character did **Peter Finch** portray in *Far From the Madding Crowd* ('67)?

W Who was dubbed **The King**?

X Who portrayed **Trixie Delight** in *Paper Moon* ('73)?

Y By which name was **William Henry Pratt** better known?

Z Name **Robert Keith's** actor son.

68 The Movie Makers: François Truffaut
Specialist; worth 4 points each

A With which school of film-makers were his early movies associated?

B Name his début movie.

C Who portrayed the women in the lives of both **Oskar Werner** and **Henry Serre** in *Jules and Jim* ('61)?

D Under which category did *Day for Night* win an Academy Award in 1973?

E Which character did he play in *Close Encounters of the Third Kind* ('77)?

69 The Movie Makers: John Schlesinger
Specialist; worth 4 points each

A Where and when was he born?

B Which university did he attend?

C Name the 16mm amateur film he directed which included actor **Robert Hardy** in the cast.

D For which 1969 movie did he win the Best Director Oscar?

E Which single player appeared in his *Billy Liar* ('63), *Darling* ('65) and *Far From the Madding Crowd* ('67)?

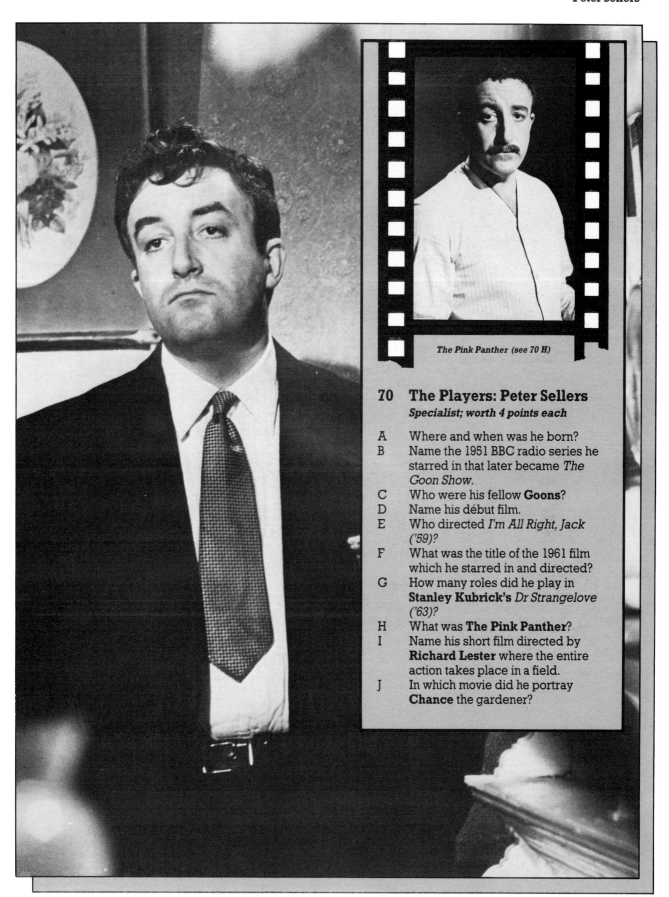

The Pink Panther (see 70 H)

70 The Players: Peter Sellers
Specialist; worth 4 points each

A   Where and when was he born?

B   Name the 1951 BBC radio series he starred in that later became *The Goon Show*.

C   Who were his fellow **Goons**?

D   Name his début film.

E   Who directed *I'm All Right, Jack* ('59)?

F   What was the title of the 1961 film which he starred in and directed?

G   How many roles did he play in **Stanley Kubrick's** *Dr Strangelove* ('63)?

H   What was **The Pink Panther**?

I   Name his short film directed by **Richard Lester** where the entire action takes place in a field.

J   In which movie did he portray **Chance** the gardener?

The Sting (see 71 I)

71 The Players: Robert Redford
Specialist; worth 4 points each

A What is his full name?
B Where and when was he born?
C Name his début movie.
D **Jane Fonda** has appeared with **Redford** in three movies, name them.
E An actor who appeared in his début movie would later direct him, who is he?
F In which 1966 movie was **Charles Bronson** a co-star?
G How many days had the **Condor**?
H Which 1970 movie reunited him with the writer and the director of *Butch Cassidy and the Sundance Kid ('69)*; who were they?
I Who did he claim influenced him in his characterisation of **Johnny Hooker** in *The Sting ('73)*?
J Name the movies in which he portrayed these characters:
  1 **Paul Bratter**
  2 **John Dortmunder**
  3 **David Chapellet**
  4 **Bill McKay**
  5 **Sonny Steele**

72 The Movie Makers: Dustin Hoffman
Specialist; worth 4 points each

A Where and when was he born?
B Name his début movie.
C Who directed *The Graduate* ('67)?
D In which movie did he portray the character **Louis Dega**?
E Who portrayed his brother in *Marathon Man* ('76)?

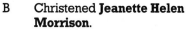

Mystery Star 12
Clues are set on a diminishing points' scale with (a) worth 5 and (e) worth 1.

A Male, born Buenos Aires, January 9 1915.
B Won the 1937 South American free-style swimming championships.
C Made his Hollywood movie début in 1951.
D Had a successful run on Broadway with **Ethel Merman** in *Happy Hunting*.
E His movies include: *The Merry Widow* ('52), *Rose Marie* ('54), *The Lost World* ('60) and *Powder Keg* ('71).

Mystery Star 13
Clues are set on a diminishing points' scale with (a) worth 5 and (e) worth 1.

A Female, born San Antonio, Texas, March 23 1904.
B Christened **Lucille Le Seuer**.
C Joined a vaudeville company in 1922 and known for a time as **Billie Cassin**.
D One-time wife of **Douglas Fairbanks Jr**.
E Her movies include: *The Boob* ('25), *Grand Hotel* ('32), *Mildred Pierce* ('45) and *Whatever Happened to Baby Jane?* ('62).

Mystery Star 14
Clues are set on a diminishing points' scale with (a) worth 5 and (e) worth 1.

A Female, born Merced, Calif., July 6 1927.

B Christened **Jeanette Helen Morrison**.
C Appeared in her first major movie role at the age of twenty.
D Two of her husbands were band leader **Stanley Reams** and actor **Tony Curtis**.
E Her movies include: *That Forsyte Woman* ('49), *The Vikings* ('58), *Psycho* ('60) and *One is a Lonely Number* ('72).

Dustin Hoffman (see 72)

73 The Movie Makers: Gene Hackman
Specialist; worth 4 points each

A Where was he born?
B Which character did he portray in *Bonnie and Clyde* ('67)?
C Name the movie in which he portrayed **Eugene Claire**.
D Who directed *Scarecrow* ('73)?
E How many times has he portrayed **Popeye Doyle** and in which movies?

Gene Hackman (see 73)

74 The Movie Makers: George Segal
Specialist; worth 4 points each

A Where and when was he born?
B Name his début movie.
C Who did he marry on November 19 1956?
D In which movie did he portray the character **Gordon Hocheiser**?
E Name his first movie with **Glenda Jackson**.

George Segal (see 74)

75 The Movie Makers: Woody Allen
Specialist; worth 4 points each

A Where and when was he born?
B By which name was he originally known?
C Name his début movie.
D How many Oscars did *Annie Hall* ('77) receive?
E In which movie did he portray the character **Isaac Davis**?

Woody Allen (see 75)

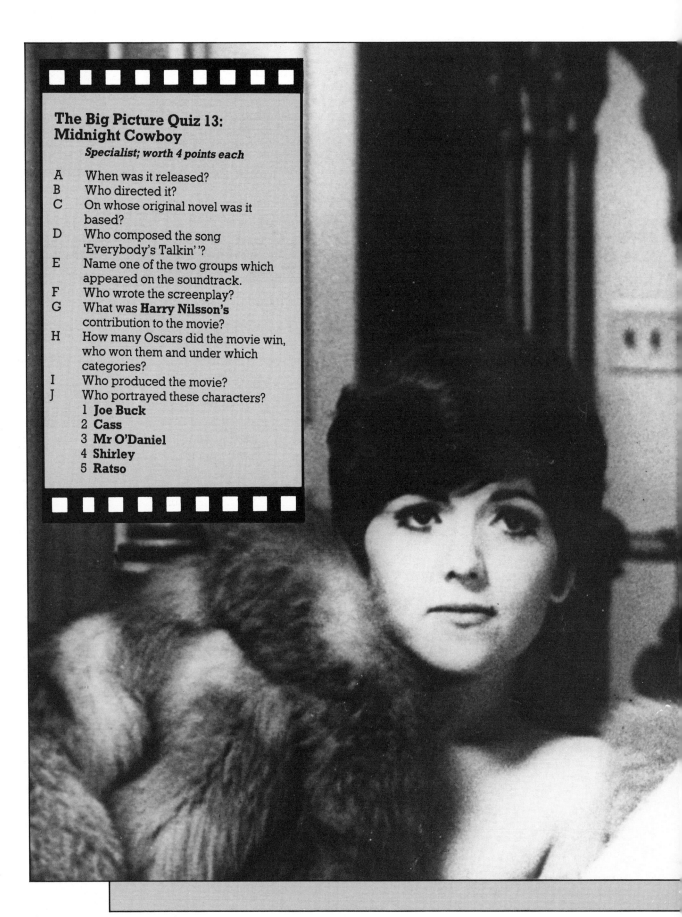

The Big Picture Quiz 13: Midnight Cowboy

Specialist; worth 4 points each

A   When was it released?
B   Who directed it?
C   On whose original novel was it based?
D   Who composed the song 'Everybody's Talkin'?
E   Name one of the two groups which appeared on the soundtrack.
F   Who wrote the screenplay?
G   What was **Harry Nilsson's** contribution to the movie?
H   How many Oscars did the movie win, who won them and under which categories?
I   Who produced the movie?
J   Who portrayed these characters?
   1 **Joe Buck**
   2 **Cass**
   3 **Mr O'Daniel**
   4 **Shirley**
   5 **Ratso**

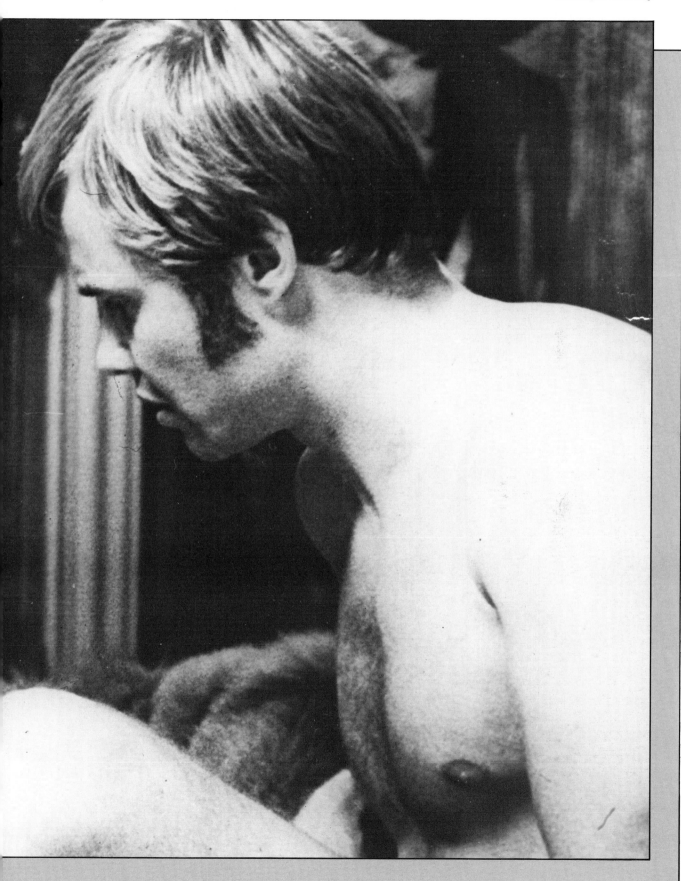

A Fistful of Dollars (see 76 E)

76 The Players: Clint Eastwood
Specialist; worth 4 points each

A What is his full name?

B Where and when was he born?

C Name his début movie.

D Which character did he portray in the TV series *Rawhide* *('58–'65)*?

E When did he make *A Fistful of Dollars* and who directed it?

F Which 1967 movie did he make under the direction of **Vittorio de Sica**?

G Name the movie which marked his return to American westerns.

H Who directed *Where Eagles Dare* *('69)*?

I **Don Siegel** who directed such classics as *Coogan's Bluff* *('68)*, *Two Mules for Sister Sara* *('69)* and *Dirty Harry* *('72)* also appeared in a cameo role in the film that introduced **Clint** as a director; name the film and the character **Siegel** portrayed.

J Name the movies in which he portrayed these characters:
1 **John McBurney**
2 **Kelly**
3 **Pardner**
4 **Harry Callahan**
5 **Ben Shockley**

Mystery Star 15

Clues are set on a diminishing points' scale with (a) worth 5 and (e) worth 1.

A   Male, born Cincinnati, Ohio, November 5 1912.
B   Christened **Leonard Slye**.
C   Appeared with the **Sons of the Pioneers** western swing group.
D   Starred in his own TV series 1952–54.
E   His movies include: *The Carson City Kid ('40), Along The Navajo Trail ('46), Night Time in Nevada ('49)* and *Son of Paleface ('52).*

77 Screen Test

General; worth 2 points each

A   Who said 'The moving picture, although a growth of only a few years, is boundless in its scope and endless in its possibilities...'?
B   Which character did **Henry Fonda** portray in *The Grapes of Wrath ('39)*?
C   Who composed the music score for *Things to Come ('35)*?
D   How much was **Louis B. Mayer** reported to have earned in 1945: £84,000, £227,000 or £104,700?
E   Who directed?
    1 *The Battleship Potemkin ('25)*
    2 *The Road to Life ('31)*
    3 *Lichtertanz ('32)*
    4 *The Last Will of Dr Mabuse ('33)*
    5 *The True Glory ('45)*
F   Which 1932 United Artists release was tagged the first great gangster picture?
G   Who said in his dying gasp 'Rosebud'?
H   Name the movie in which **Anthony Quinn** portrayed an Eskimo.
I   In *American Graffiti ('73)* who portrayed?
    1 **Curt**
    2 **Steve**
    3 **Debbie**
    4 **John**
    5 **Laurie**
J   Which husband and wife team appeared in *Murphy's War ('71)*?
K   How old was **Barry Fitzgerald** when he became a professional actor?

L   By which name was **Maria Jurado Garcia** better known?
M   What was the title of **Sally Kellerman's** début movie?
N   Which sport was featured in **Bruce Brown's** *The Endless Summer ('66)*?
O   Who was **Andrew McLaglen's** actor father?
P   Which 1967 movie featured the bluegrass tune 'Foggy Mountain Breakdown'?
Q   Who played the leading roles in *X Y and Zee* (or *Zee and Co.*) *('72)*?
R   Who was nicknamed **La Lollo**?
S   In 1955 **Susan Hayward, Katharine Hepburn, Jennifer Jones, Anna Magnani** and **Eleanor Parker** were all nominated for the Best Actress Academy Award. Who won?
T   Name **Bud Abbott's** partner after his break-up with **Lou Costello**.
U   Who directed *The Maltese Falcon ('31)*?
V   Which 1966 movie included the characters **Willie Garvin** and **Gabriel**?
W   What is the title of director **Steve Ihnat's** only movie?
X   *Town Without Pity ('61)* and *Private Property ('61)* dealt with which offence?
Y   Who portrayed **Minnie** and **Moskowitz** in the film of the same name?
Z   In which movie did **Burt Reynolds** portray 87th Precinct detective **Steve Carella**?

Burt Reynolds (see 77 Z)

American Graffiti (see 77 I)

Star Couple 8
General; worth 2 points each

Identify this 'on and off' screen couple.

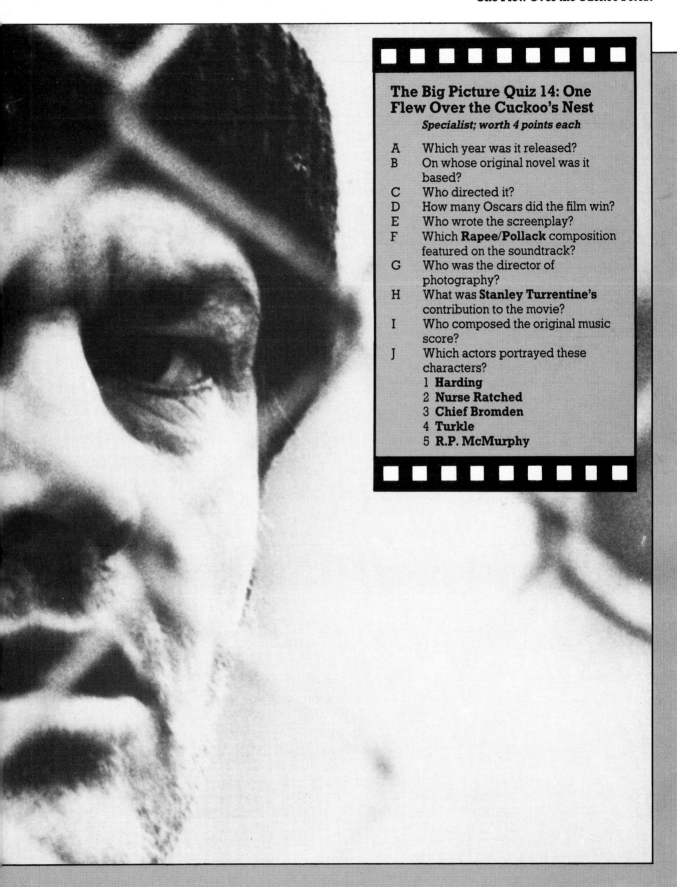

The Big Picture Quiz 14: One Flew Over the Cuckoo's Nest

Specialist; worth 4 points each

A   Which year was it released?
B   On whose original novel was it based?
C   Who directed it?
D   How many Oscars did the film win?
E   Who wrote the screenplay?
F   Which **Rapee/Pollack** composition featured on the soundtrack?
G   Who was the director of photography?
H   What was **Stanley Turrentine's** contribution to the movie?
I   Who composed the original music score?
J   Which actors portrayed these characters?
   1 **Harding**
   2 **Nurse Ratched**
   3 **Chief Bromden**
   4 **Turkle**
   5 **R.P. McMurphy**

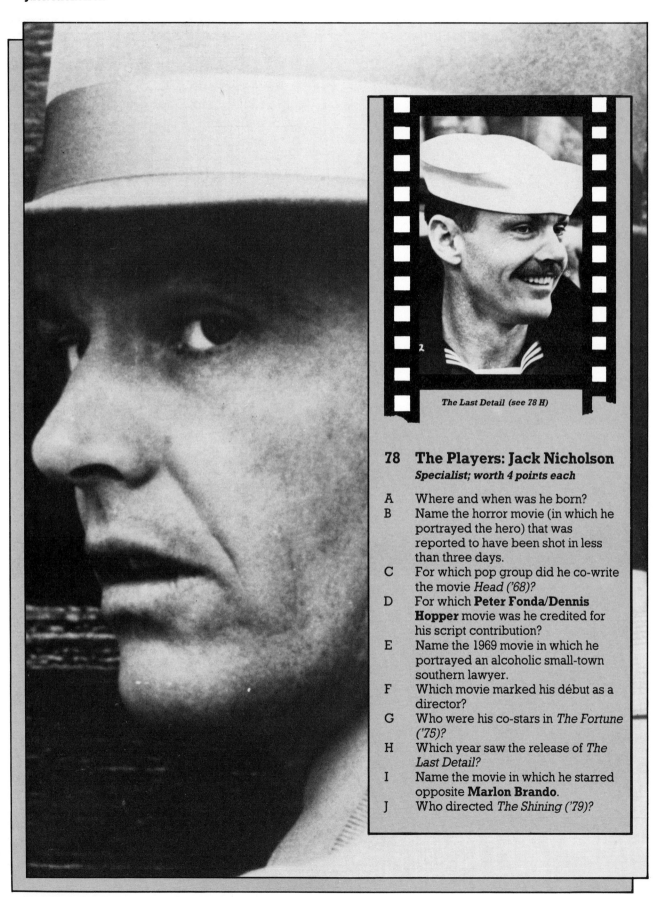

The Last Detail (see 78 H)

78 The Players: Jack Nicholson
Specialist; worth 4 points each

A   Where and when was he born?

B   Name the horror movie (in which he portrayed the hero) that was reported to have been shot in less than three days.

C   For which pop group did he co-write the movie *Head* ('68)?

D   For which **Peter Fonda/Dennis Hopper** movie was he credited for his script contribution?

E   Name the 1969 movie in which he portrayed an alcoholic small-town southern lawyer.

F   Which movie marked his début as a director?

G   Who were his co-stars in *The Fortune* ('75)?

H   Which year saw the release of *The Last Detail?*

I   Name the movie in which he starred opposite **Marlon Brando**.

J   Who directed *The Shining* ('79)?

Mystery Star 16

Clues are set on a diminishing points' scale with (a) worth 5 and (e) worth 1.

A Female, born Berlin, December 27 1902.

B Christened **Maria Magdalena Von Losch**.

C Appeared in the 1929 revue *Zwei Kravatten*.

D Spent much of World War II entertaining allied troops.

E Her movies include: *Desire* ('32), *Seven Sinners* ('40), *Witness for the Prosecution* ('58) and *Judgment at Nuremberg* ('61).

Mystery Star 17

Clues are set on a diminishing points' scale with (a) worth 5 and (e) worth 1.

A Male, born St Louis, Miss., May 27 1911.

B Started his acting career in London.

C Highly rated as both an art historian and gourmet cook.

D His autobiography was published under the title *I Like What I Know*.

E His movies include: *Elizabeth and Essex* ('39), *The Three Musketeers* ('49), *The Fall of the House of Usher* ('61) and *Theatre of Blood* ('73).

Mystery Star 18

Clues are set on a diminishing points' scale with (a) worth 5 and (e) worth 1.

A Female, born Lowell, Mass., May 5 1908.

B Performed with the **Provincetown Players**.

C Made her Broadway début in 1929.

D Husbands have included **William Grant Sherry** and **Gary Merrill**.

E Her movies include: *Cabin in the Cotton* ('32), *Deception* ('46), *Dead Ringer* ('64) and *Bunny O'Hare* ('71).

Mystery Star 19

Clues are set on a diminishing points' scale with (a) worth 5 and (e) worth 1.

A Female, born Philadelphia, Pa., November 12 1928.

B Studied drama at the American Academy of Dramatic Arts.

C Made her Broadway début in *The*

Film Poster 4
General; worth 2 points each

Give the title of the film this poster is advertising.

Star Couple 9
General; worth 2 points each

Identify this 'on and off' screen couple.

Father ('49).

D Her brother **Jack** became one of TVs *Mavericks* while she became a princess.

E Her movies include: *High Noon* ('52), *Rear Window* ('54), *To Catch A Thief* ('55) and *High Society* ('56).

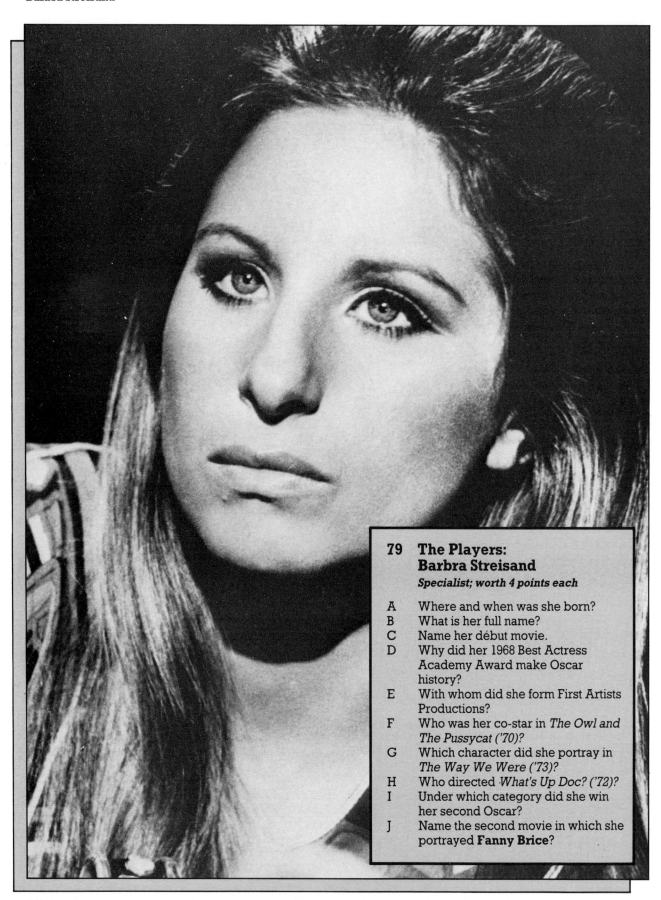

**79   The Players:
Barbra Streisand**
Specialist; worth 4 points each

A   Where and when was she born?
B   What is her full name?
C   Name her début movie.
D   Why did her 1968 Best Actress
    Academy Award make Oscar
    history?
E   With whom did she form First Artists
    Productions?
F   Who was her co-star in *The Owl and
    The Pussycat* ('70)?
G   Which character did she portray in
    The Way We Were ('73)?
H   Who directed *What's Up Doc?* ('72)?
I   Under which category did she win
    her second Oscar?
J   Name the second movie in which she
    portrayed **Fanny Brice**?

80 Screen Test

General; worth 2 points each

A Name four out of the seven actresses who portrayed the 'birds' in *Alfie* ('66).

B Who portrayed **Jason Love** in *Where the Spies Are* ('65)?

C What was the title of the love theme featured in *The Deer Hunter* ('78) and who composed it?

D Who is known simply as **BB**?

E By which names were **David Daniel Kaminsky** and **Melvin Kaminsky** better known?

F What is **Richard Chamberlain's** full name?

G In 1968 **Alan Arkin, Ron Moody, Peter O'Toole, Cliff Robertson** and **Alan Bates** were all nominated for the Best Actor Academy Award; who won?

H Who directed the **Funicello/Avalon** *Beach Party* series?

I In *Rocky* ('76) who portrayed?

Star Couple 10
General; worth 2 points each

Identify this 'on and off' screen couple.

1 **Adrian**
2 **Mickey**
3 **Paulie**
4 **Apollo**
5 **Rocky**

J What nationality is **Fernando Rey**?

K Who portrayed **Jesus** in *King of Kings* ('61)?

L What is **Al Pacino's** full name?

M Who wrote the original stories of *The Guns of Navarone* ('60), *When Eight Bells Toll* ('70) and *Puppet on a Chain* ('71)?

N Who composed the music for?
1 *The Pawnbroker* ('65)
2 *In Cold Blood* ('67)
3 *MacKenna's Gold* ('69)
4 *Up Tight* ('68)
5 *The Anderson Tapes* ('72)

O What have **Sandra Dee, Deborah Walley** and **Cindy Carol** in common?

P Who portrayed **Enrico Caruso** in *The Great Caruso* ('50)?

Q Which character did **Marlene Dietrich** portray in *The Blue Angel* ('30)?

R Who directed *A Man for All Seasons* ('66)?

S Who was the founder of Universal Pictures?

T From which novel was *The Uninvited* ('43) adapted?

U Name **Helen Hayes'** actor son.

V Who was the voice behind **Sylvester** the cartoon cat?

W What have **Lionel Barrymore, Harry Baur, Edmund Purdom, Christopher Lee, Gert Frobe** and **Tom Baker** in common?

X Which 1941 movie was based on **Geoffrey Household's** *Rogue Male*?

Y In the 1922 version who portrayed **Little Lord Fauntleroy**?

Z Name the 1942 film written and directed by **Leslie Howard** about inventor of the Spitfire **R.J. Mitchell**.

Alan Arkin (see 80 G)

Beach Party (see 80 H)

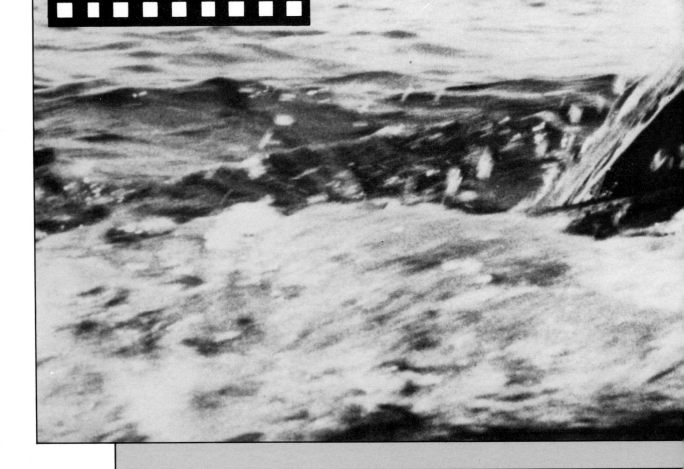

The Big Picture Quiz 15: Jaws
Specialist; worth 4 points each

A   Which year was it released?
B   Who directed it?
C   On whose original novel was it based?
D   Where was most of the action shot?
E   What was **John Williams'** contribution to the movie?
F   Who wrote the screenplay?
G   What was the name of the fictitious Long Island town where the adventure was set?
H   Who portrayed these characters?
   1 **Brody**
   2 **Vaughn**
   3 **Hooper**
   4 **Quint**
   5 **Ellen Brody**
I   What was the monster at the centre of the story?
J   Name the sequel.

Mystery Star 20

Clues are set on a diminishing points' scale with (a) worth 5 and (e) worth 1.

A   Male, born Macon, Georgia, April 5 1905.

B   The son of concert pianist **Edward Hesselberg**.

C   Married **Helen Gahagen**.

D   Became the first actor to be a delegate to a national convention.

E   His movies include: *As You Desire Me* ('32), *The Sea of Grass* ('47), *Hud* ('63), *The Candidate* ('72) and *Being There* ('80).

Mystery Star 21

Clues are set on a diminishing points' scale with (a) worth 5 and (e) worth 1.

A   Female, born Paris, September 13 1905.

B   Moved to the US in 1913.

C   Studied art in New York.

D   Made her Broadway début in 1924.

E   Her movies include: *Three Cornered Moon* ('33), *Arise My Love* ('40), *The Planter's Wife* ('52) and *Parrish* ('60).

Mystery Star 22

Clues are set on a diminishing points' scale with (a) worth 5 and (e) worth 1.

A   Female, born Brooklyn, New York, January 3 1900.

B   Christened **Marion Douras**.

C   Made her stage début in *Chu Chin Chow* ('34).

D   Appeared in the *Ziegfeld Follies*.

E   Her movies include: *The Dark Star* ('19), *The Red Mill* ('25), *Peg o' My Heart* ('33) and *Ever Since Eve* ('37).

Film Poster 5

General; worth 2 points each   Give the title of the film this poster is advertising.

THE ANSWERS

1 Screen Test
(A) Jack L., Albert, Harry M. & Sam (B) Six (C) Jack Lemmon & Walter Matthau (D) The Singer Not the Song ('60) (E) 1 Zero Mostel, Gene Wilder 2 Burt Lancaster, Kirk Douglas 3 Dustin Hoffman, Jon Voight 4 Paul Newman, Robert Redford 5 Tony Curtis, Charles Bronson (F) She (G) Robert Redford (H) Seventy-six (I) Sex and the Single Girl ('64) (J) German (K) High Anxiety (L) 1, 2, 3, & 5 John Williams 4 Neal Hefti (M) Rita Hayworth (N) David, Keith & Robert Carradine, James & Stacy Keach, Dennis & Randy Quaid, Christopher & Nicholas Guest (O) Mary Martin (P) Who's Afraid of Virginia Woolf? ('66) (Q) A leopard (R) Omar Sharif, Cinderella – Italian Style ('67), Dr Zhivago ('65), Mackenna's Gold ('68) (S) Jane Fonda (T) Sitting Pretty ('48) (U) Nick Charles, The Thin Man (V) Peter Lorre (W) 1,2,4 & 5 Don Siegel 3 Clint Eastwood (X) Bruce (Y) Connie Francis (Z) Inside Daisy Clover ('66), This Property is Condemned ('66), The Candidate ('72)

2 The Players: Charles Chaplin
(A) Walworth, London, April 16 1889 (B) Fred Karno's troupe (C) 1910 (D) Mack Sennett (E) Making A Living ('14) (F) Kid Auto Races at Venice ('14), Henry Lehrman (G) Sixteen (H) Jackie Coogan (I) 1936 (J) Seventy-seventh

3 The Pioneers
(A) Mrs Harvey Henderson Wilcox (B) David Wark (C) April 17 1919 (D) Lon Chaney (E) John Gilbert (F) Pickfair (G) 1923 (H) Clara Bow (I) Raoul Walsh, Donald Crisp, 1915 (J) 1912, Mack Sennett (K) A Woman of Paris ('23) (L) Will Rogers (M) Tramp, Tramp, Tramp ('26) (N) Harold Lloyd (O) Fritz Lang (P) Bela Blasko (Q) D.W. Griffith (R) Anna May Wong (S) H.B. Warner (T) Hans Erich Maria Stroheim von Nordenwall (U) Ben Turpin (V) 1924 (W) Barbara La Marr (X) Marie Dressler & Wallace Beery (Y) The Fugitive ('13) (Z) 1927

4 The Players: Rudolph Valentino
(A) Castellaneta, Southern Italy, May 6 1895 (B) Rodolfo Alfonzo Rafaelo Pierre Filibert Guglielmi di Valentino (C) December 1913 (D) Jean Acker (E) Julio Desnoyers (F) Adolph Zukor (G) October 1921 (H) Mexico, May 13 1922 (I) J.D. Williams (J) Son of the Sheik ('26), George Fitzmaurice

5 Screen Test
(A) Sam Goldwyn (B) John Ford (C) Jean-Louis Trintignant & Anouk Aimée (D) Targets ('68) (E) Tony Curtis, The Great Imposter (F) Sean Connery, David Niven, George Lazenby, Roger Moore (G) Laurence Olivier, Marathon Man (H) Spartacus, 'I'm Spartacus' (I) Richard Burton (J) All have portrayed Tarzan (K) Mae Clarke (L) Ecstasy (M) Sessue Hayakawa (N) Sunset Boulevard (O) Ray Milland (P) It Happened One Night (Q) John Wayne (R) In Search of the Castaways ('63) (S) Paul Newman & Joanne Woodward (T) Henry Fonda (U) The Four Just Men ('59) (V) Jean Harlow (W) Gladys Aylward (X) Gabriel Dell, Bobby Jordan, Leo Gorcey, Huntz Hall, Bernard Punsley, Bill Halop (Y) The Waldorf (Z) 1 Sidney Poitier, Rod Steiger 2 Peter Finch, Jane Fonda, Angela Lansbury

6 Stage Names
(A) Kirk Douglas (B) Rock Hudson (C) Mary Pickford (D) Michael Caine (E) Yves Montand (F) Lana Turner (G) Troy Donahue (H) Robert Taylor (I) Richard Burton (J) Omar Sharif (K) Sandra Dee (L) Jeff Chandler (M) Cyd Charisse (N) Charles Bronson (O) Craig Stevens (P) Michael Callan (Q) Paula Prentiss (R) Ethel Merman (S) Lee J. Cobb (T) Jeffrey Hunter (U) John Wayne (V) Elke Sommer (W)

89

George Burns (X) Maureen O'Hara (Y) Rita Moreno (Z) Walter Matthau

7 The Players: Greta Garbo
(A) Stockholm, September 18 1905 (B) Greta Gustafson (C) Mauritz Stiller (D) Peter the Tramp ('22) (E) 1925 (F) Flesh and the Devil ('27) (G) Love ('28) (H) Clarence Brown, Anna Christie ('30) (I) John Barrymore (J) Nancy Kelly

8 Screen Test
(A) Groucho, Harpo, Chico & Zeppo (B) Casablanca (C) The Titanic (D) Oliver Reed (E) 1 Aurora Miranda 2 Mijanou Bardot 3 Marisa Pavan 4 Juliet Mills 5 Lana Wood (F) Lust For Life ('56) (G) Frank Perry (H) Network ('76) (I) James Coburn, Charles Bronson & John Leyton (J) Anna and the King of Siam (K) Happy Days (L) Gene Hackman (M) 1 James Caan, Alan Arkin 2 Clark Gable, Burt Lancaster 3 Elliot Gould, Donald Sutherland 4 John Wayne, Kirk Douglas 5 Elliot Gould, George Segal (N) Judy Garland, Mickey Rooney (O) Beloved Infidel ('59) (P) Stanley Kubrick (Q) Joseph Wambaugh (R) Cheyenne Autumn ('64) (S) Edward Fox (T) The Defiant Ones ('58) (U) Lloyd Bridges (V) Carroll Baker (W) François Truffaut (X) D'Ascoynes (Y) Frank Sinatra (Z) 1 Errol Flynn 2 Olivia de Havilland 3 Claude Rains 4 Basil Rathbone

9 The Movie Makers: Laurel and Hardy
(A) Ulverston, Lancs., June 16 1890 (B) Arthur Stanley Jefferson (C) Harlem Ga., January 18 1892 (D) 1926 (E) 1960

10 The Players: Spencer Tracy
(A) Milwaukee, Wisc., April 5 1900 (B) Spencer Bonaventure Tracy (C) Taxi Talks ('30) (D) John Ford (E) San Francisco ('36) (F) Ingrid Bergman (G) Nine (H) Sir Cedric Hardwicke (I) Bad Day at Black Rock (J) 1 Guess Who's Coming to Dinner ('67) 2 The Devil at Four O'Clock ('61) 3 Adam's Rib ('49) 4 Edison the Man ('40) 5 Boys' Town ('38)

11 Title Roles
(A) Ernest Borgnine (B) Robert Culp, Natalie Wood, Elliot Gould, Dyan Cannon (C) Dirk Bogarde (D) Dustin Hoffman, Mia Farrow (E) Greta Garbo (F) Michael Caine (G) Spencer Tracy, Katharine Hepburn (H) Faye Dunaway, Warren Beatty (I) Robby Benson (J) Leslie Caron (K) Cliff Robertson (L) Sean Connery, Audrey Hepburn (M) A rat (N) Ewa Aulin (O) Walter Matthau, Carol Burnett (P) James Coburn (Q) Dorothy McGuire, Robert Young (R) Sissy Spacek (S) Lucille Ball (T) Clark Gable, Marion Davies (U) Peter Boyle (V) Keir Dullea, Janet Margolin (W) Sylvester Stallone (X) Elizabeth Taylor (Y) Tippi Hedren (Z) Silvana Mangano

12 Screen Test
(A) Robert Altman (B) Adam Roarke (C) 1972 (D) Frank Sinatra (E) 1, 2, 3 & 5 Francis Lai 4 Georges Delerue (F) The Little Prince (G) Tom Robinson (H) Laslo Benedek (I) Shelley Winters (J) Kid Galahad (K) Michael Redgrave (L) Bette Davis (M) Korean War (N) Phffft (O) Loss of Innocence (P) 1 Fred Astaire 2 Cyd Charisse 3 Jack Buchanan 4 Oscar Levant 5 Nanette Fabray (Q) All in Good Time (R) 108 minutes (S) Sally Bowles (T) Monty Norman (U) The Outlaw (V) James Fox (W) Diana Fluck (X) 1 Judy Garland 2 Ray Bolger 3 Jack Haley 4 Bert Lahr 5 Frank Morgan (Y) The Wiz (Z) All have portrayed Sexton Blake

13 The Players: Clark Gable
(A) Cadiz, Ohio, February 1 1901 (B) William Clark Gable (C) Rex Jewel, manager of the Astoria Stock Company (D) It Happened One Night (E) Jack Warner (F) March 1939 (G) Major (H) Adventure ('45) (I) John Huston, The Misfits ('61) (J) 1 Rhett Butler 2 Fletcher Christian 3 Blackie Norton 4 Jim Lane 5 Big John McMasters

14 The Movie Makers: Cecil B. de Mille
(A) Ashfield, Mass., August 12 1881 (B) Cecil Blount de Mille (C) The Squaw Man ('13) (D) Sam Goldwyn & Jesse L. Lasky (E) Sunset Boulevard ('50)

15 The Movie Makers: Fred Astaire
(A) Omaha, Neb., May 10 1899 (B) Frederick Austerlitz (C) His sister Adèle (D) Dancing Lady ('33) (E) Flying Down to Rio ('33)

16 Screen Test
(A) Anne Bancroft (B) Lady in a Cage ('64) (C) Assam Province, India (D) Skidoo ('68) (E) Lex Barker (F) Chester Riley (G) Cliff 'Ukelele Ike' Edwards (H) The Westerner ('38) (I) 1 Queen Elizabeth ('12) 2 The Virgin Queen ('55) 3 Fire Over England ('36) 4 The Private Lives of Elizabeth and Essex ('39) 5 Young Bess ('53) 6 Drake of England ('35) (J) Bulldog Drummond (K) Macdonald Carey (L) Yellow Submarine ('68) (M) Frank Lloyd Wright (N) Irish (O) 1940 (P) Kenneth More (Q) Dentist (R) Brian De Palma (S) Port of New York ('50) (T) Nashville (U) Jacqueline Bisset (V) Innocents in Paris ('29) (W) Jealous Lover, Equilibrium & Mademoiselle (X) Miss West Seattle (Y) 1,2,3 & 5 Lalo Schifrin 4 Jerry Fielding (Z) Peter Sellers, Alan Arkin

17 The Movie Makers: James Cagney
(A) New York City, July 17 1899 (B) James Francis Cagney Jr (C) Sinner's Holiday ('30) (D) Bottom (E) Yankee Doodle Dandy ('42)

18 The Movie Makers: Edward G. Robinson
(A) Emanuel Goldenberg (B) Rumania (C) Little Caesar (D) The Whole Town's Talking ('34), Cheyenne Autumn ('64) (E) Dr Max Stratman

19 The Players: Humphrey Bogart
(A) New York City, December 25 1899 (B) Humphrey DeForest Bogart (C) Navy (D) Helen Menken (E) A Devil with Women ('30) (F) Edward G. Robinson (G) George Brent, Ray Milland, Dick Powell (H) To Have and Have Not ('45) (I) Charlie Allnut in The African

Queen (J) 1 The Treasure of the Sierra Madre ('47) 2 The Big Sleep ('46) 3 The Caine Mutiny ('54) 4 High Sierra ('41) 5 The Maltese Falcon ('41)

20 Stage Names

(A) Natalie Wood (B) Robert Blake (C) Woody Allen (D) Mel Brooks (E) Jayne Mansfield (F) John Saxon (G) Jane Russell (H) Raquel Welch (I) Nick Adams (J) Eddie Albert (K) June Allyson (L) Dana Andrews (M) Richard Arlen (N) Robert Armstrong (O) Fred Astaire (P) Lauren Bacall (Q) Gene Barry (R) Fredric March (S) Shirley Maclaine (T) Dirk Bogarde (U) Gig Young (V) Raymond St Jacques (W) Randolph Scott (X) Alice Faye (Y) Jill St John (Z) Catherine Deneuve

21 Screen Test

(A) Al, Jim & Harry (B) Luis Buñuel (C) Singapore (D) Alice's Restaurant (E) Ninety-two (F) Nevada Smith (G) TV comedy writer (H) 1 Richard Gere 2 Lisa Eichhorn 3 Vanessa Redgrave 4 Chick Vennara 5 William Devane (I) Lloyd Vernet Bridges (J) Tom Conway (K) Claudette Colbert (L) The Chase ('65) (M) Max Steiner (N) Liza Minnelli (O) Charlotte Vale, Jerry Durrance (P) Lilith ('64) (Q) Elmer Gantry ('60) (R) The Robe ('53) Henri Chrétien (S) Mario Lanza (T) James Bond (U) Orson Welles (V) Rhapsody In Blue (W) Cleavon Little (X) Ilya Kuriakin (Y) Michael Douglas (Z) Sixty-one

22 The Players: Carole Lombard

(A) Fort Wayne, Ind., October 6 1909 (B) Jane Alice Peters (C) A Perfect Crime ('21) (D) An automobile accident (E) Mack Sennett (F) William Powell (G) Gregory La Cava (H) March 1939 (I) Robert Montgomery (J) To Be Or Not To Be ('42)

23 Child's Play

(A) Billy Chapin & Sally Jane Bruce (B) Santa Monica, Calif., April 23 1928 (C) Kevin Corcoran (D) Member of the Wedding ('52) (E) Alan Barnes & Diana Holdgate (F) Darryl Hickman (G) Lassie (H) Jackie Cooper (I) Never A Dull Moment (J) Baby Sandy (K) George Winslow (L) Green (M) Johnny Sheffield (N) The Proud Rebel (O) 1961 (P) Jimmy Bean (Q) Curly (R) Shane (S) Philippe Delacy (T) Donna Corcoran (U) Ted Donaldson (V) Billy Chapin (W) Tomorrow is Forever ('46) (X) Justin Dreyfuss (Y) Best Supporting Actress (Z) Bugsy Malone ('76)

24 The Movie Makers: Alfred Hitchcock

(A) The Pleasure Garden ('25) (B) 1939 (C) Blackmail ('29) (D) Hilton A. Green (E) Frenzy ('72)

25 The Movie Makers: Billy Wilder

(A) Vienna, June 22 1906 (B) Journalist (C) Mauvaise Graine ('33) (D) Charles Brackett (E) Three, Best Film (producer), Best Direction, Best Story & Screenplay (with I.A.L. Diamond)

26 The Players: John Wayne

(A) Winterset, Iowa, May 26 1907 (B) Marion Michael Morrison (C) Raoul Walsh (D) The Long Voyage Home ('40) (E) Esperanza Baner (F) Ireland (G) The Alamo (H) Rooster Cogburn, True Grit ('69) (I) The Shootist ('76) (J) 1 Thomas Danson 2 Captain Nathan Brittles 3 Lt. Col. Kirby York 4 Ethan Edwards 5 Sheriff John T. Chance

27 Western Round-up

(A) 1 Randolph Scott 2 Henry Fonda 3 Burt Lancaster 4 James Garner 5 Harris Yulin (B) 1 Gary Cooper 2 Bruce Cabot 3 Reed Hadley 4 Forrest Tucker 5 Howard Keel (C) 1 Clayton Moore 2 Jay Silverheels Jr 3 Perry Lopez 4 Michael Ansara 5 Lyle Bettger (D) William Wyler (E) The True Story of Jesse James ('57) (F) Yul Brynner, Steve McQueen, Charles Bronson, James Coburn, Robert Vaughn, Horst Buchholz, Brad Dexter (G) Calvera (H) 1 Elmer Bernstein 2 Bronislau Kaper 3 Ennio Morricone 4 Jerome Moross 5 Jerry Goldsmith (I) Wounded Knee Creek (J) John Milius & Edward Anhalt (K) Victor

Jory (L) Tony (M) The Sheepman ('58) (N) Jack Lemmon (O) Walter Brennan (P) Victoria Princepal, Steve Kanaly (Q) 1 Richard Boone 2 Laurence Harvey 3 Richard Widmark 4 John Wayne 5 Ken Curtis (R) John Huston (S) Dolores Hart (T) Lee Marvin (U) 1962 (V) Will Penny ('67) (W) Sergio Leone (X) Cat Ballou ('65) (Y) The Nine Lives of Elfego Baca ('59) (Z) Howard Hughes

28 The Movie Makers: James Stewart

(A) Indiana, Pa., May 20 1908 (B) James Maitland Stewart (C) The Murder Man ('35), Shorty (D) The Philadelphia Story ('40) (E) 1 Monty Stratton 2 Elwood P. Dowd 3 Charles Lindbergh 4 Grant McLaine 5 Wyatt Earp

29 The Movie Makers: Robert Mitchum

(A) Bridgeport, Conn., August 6 1917 (B) Hoppy Serves A Writ ('43) (C) Ballad of Thunder Road (D) Australia (E) David Lean

30 The Players: Kirk Douglas

(A) Amsterdam, New York, December 9 1916 (B) Issur Danielovitch Demsky (C) The Strange Love of Martha Ivers ('46) (D) Stanley Kramer (E) The Big Carnival (F) The Bad and The Beautiful (G) Twenty Thousand Leagues under the Sea (H) Pretty Little Girl in the Yellow Dress (I) A Gunfight ('71) (J) 1 Lust for Life ('56) 2 Cast A Giant Shadow ('66) 3 Gunfight at the OK Corral ('57) 4 Paths of Glory ('57) 5 The Last Sunset ('61)

31 The Movie Makers: Errol Flynn

(A) Hobart, Tasmania (B) Errol Leslie Thompson Flynn (C) In the Wake of the Bounty ('33) (D) Too Much Too Soon ('58) (E) Beam Ends

32 The Movie Makers: Orson Welles

(A) Kenosha, Wisc., May 6 1915 (B) October 30 1938 (C) Too Much Johnson ('38) (D) Harry Lime (E) Best Original Screenplay (with Herman J. Mankiewicz)

33 Screen Test

(A) Fashion designer (B) Freelance illustrator (C) Gregory Peck (D) Ronald Reagan, January 20 1981 (E) Silent Movie (F) 1 Audrey Hepburn 2 Rex Harrison 3 Stanley Holloway 4 Wilfred Hyde White 5 Gladys Cooper (G) Leslie Townes Hope (H) David Niven (I) Paper Moon ('73) (J) Rodney Harrington (K) Stewart Granger (L) Richard Pryor (M) Chihuahua, Mexico (N) John Cassavetes (O) Diane Baker (P) 1,2,3 & 5 Henry Mancini 4 Marvin Hamlisch (Q) Don Juan ('26) (R) The Detective Story ('50) (S) Dress designs (T) Hyacinth Hazel O'Higgins (U) 1952 (V) Lost Horizon (W) Jeanette MacDonald (X) Meet Me in St Louis ('44) (Y) Life at the Top ('65) (Z) Ronald Searle

34 The Players: Elizabeth Taylor

(A) London, February 27 1932 (B) Elizabeth Rosemond Taylor (C) Man or Mouse ('48) (D) May 6 1950 (E) Montgomery Clift (F) Butterfield 8 (G) Vincente Minnelli (H) Budapest (I) Richard Burton (J) 1 Kay Banks 2 Kay Dunstan 3 Maggie 4 Catherine Holly 5 Mrs Flora Goforth

35 The Movie Makers: Cary Grant

(A) Bristol, Avon (B) Archibald Leach (C) This Is the Night ('32) (D) Night and Day ('45) (E) 1969

36 The Movie Makers: Rudy Vallee

(A) Island Pond, Vermont, July 28 1901 (B) Hubert Prior Vallee (C) The Vagabond Lover ('29) (D) Terry Moore (E) How to Succeed in Business without Really Trying ('67)

37 The Movie Makers: Dirk Bogarde

(A) Derek Van Den Bogaerd (B) Esther Waters ('47), William Latch (C) Barrister (D) I Could Go On Singing ('63) (E) 1 Once a Jolly Swagman ('48) 2 The Blue Lamp ('50) 3 Song Without End ('60) 4 So Long At the Fair ('49) 5 Doctor in the House ('53), Doctor at Sea ('55), Doctor at Large ('56), The Doctor's Dilemma ('59), Doctor in Distress ('64)

38 The Songs

(A) The Thomas Crown Affair ('68) (B) The Joker Is Wild ('57) (C) Gold Diggers of 35 ('35) (D) The Towering Inferno ('74) (E) Breakfast At Tiffany's ('61) (F) Swing Time ('36) (G) Butch Cassidy and the Sundance Kid ('69) (H) The Gay Divorcee ('34) (I) The Harvey Girls ('46) (J) Lovers and Other Strangers ('69) (K) Calamity Jane ('53) (L) State Fair ('45) (M) The Sandpiper ('65) (N) Hello Frisco Hello ('43) (O) A Star Is Born ('76) (P) Captain Carey USA (GB After Midnight) ('51) (Q) The Last Time I Saw Paris ('54) (R) Nashville ('75) (S) Song of the South ('74) (T) A Hole in the Head ('59) (U) Holiday Inn ('42) (V) The Man Who Knew Too Much ('56) (W) Papa's Delicate Condition ('63) (X) Neptune's Daughter ('49) (Y) Here Comes The Groom ('51) (Z) Pinocchio ('39)

39 The Movie Makers: Gregory Peck

(A) La Jolla, Calif., April 5 1916 (B) Eldred Gregory Peck (C) Days of Glory ('44) (D) Atticus Finch in To Kill a Mockingbird (E) Producer

40 The Players: Laurence Olivier

(A) Dorking, Surrey, May 22 1907 (B) Lord Laurence Kerr Olivier (C) Jill Esmond (D) Too Many Crooks ('30) (E) Friends and Lovers ('31) (F) Orlando (G) Vivien Leigh (H) Henry V ('44) (I) Two, Best Film (producer) Best Actor (J) 1 Pride and Prejudice ('40) 2 The Entertainer ('60) 3 The Beggar's Opera ('52) 4 A Bridge Too Far ('78) 5 Rebecca ('40)

41 The Players: Marilyn Monroe

(A) Los Angeles, June 1 1926 (B) Norma Jean Baker (or Mortenson) (C) Jim Dougherty (D) The Asphalt Jungle (E) Joseph L. Mankiewicz (F) Twentieth Century-Fox (G) Lee & Paula Strasberg (H) The Wrong Kind of Girl (I) Tony Curtis (J) The Misfits ('61), Arthur Miller, Roslyn

42 War Games

(A) Robert Mitchum (B) 1951 (C) Lewis Gilbert (D) Sefton (E) Colonel Bogey, K.J. Alford (F) Hardy Kruger (G) Vietnam (H) Twelve O'Clock High ('50) (I) Sergeant Reese (J) Cliff Robertson (K) 1930 (L) Seven (M) Korean (N) Violette Szabo GC (O) Richard Burton (P) The Longest Day ('61) (Q) Richard Fleischer, Toshio Masuda, Kinji Fukasaku (R) Major Reisman (Lee Marvin) (S) Ron Goodwin (T) Gregory Peck, David Niven, Anthony Quinn, Stanley Baker, Anthony Quayle & James Darren (U) Hi There!, Dear John (V) Lancashire (W) 1 George C. Scott 2 Karl Malden (X) Beer (Y) Frank Borzage (Z) M.A.S.H

43 The Players: Burt Lancaster

(A) New York City, November 2 1913 (B) Burton Stephen Lancaster (C) Nick Cravat (D) The Killers ('46) (E) Sinclair Lewis alias Elmer Gantry ('60) (F) Harold Hecht (G) Daniel Mann (H) Joe Bass (I) Scorpio ('73) (J) The Kentuckian ('55)

44 Stage Names

(A) Tony Curtis (B) Bud Spencer (C) Ray Milland (D) Jack Palance (E) Terry Moore (F) Edd 'Kookie' Byrnes (G) Anna Neagle (H) Cary Grant (I) Melvyn Douglas (J) Twiggy (K) Virginia Mayo (L) Jackie Oakie (M) Linda Christian (N) Slim Pickens (O) Merle Oberon (P) Barbara Stanwyck (Q) Cantinflas (R) Anouk Aimée (S) Don Ameche (T) Julie Andrews (U) George Arliss (V) Frankie Avalon (W) Anne Bancroft (X) Busby Berkeley (Y) Stephen Boyd (Z) Patrick Wymark

45 Screen Test

(A) Chicago, Ill. (B) Ordinary People ('80) (C) Earle (D) 1973 (E) Georgetown, Washington DC (F) Golden Boy ('39) (G) 1 James Stewart 2 June Allyson 3 Charles Drake 4 Marion Ross 5 Louis Armstrong (H) Tom Wolfe (I) Alamo (J) Nicolas Roeg & Donald Cammell (K) Tokyo (L) Photographer (M) Henry Fonda (N) 1 Richard Harris 2 David Niven 3 James Garner 4 Rock Hudson 5 Cary Grant 6 Rod

Taylor (O) Apple Annie (P) Rio De Janeiro (Q) Play It Again Sam ('72) (R) Rocky Graziano (S) 1 Chopin 2 Tchaikovsky 3 Lizst 4 Beethoven 5 Grieg (T) Son of Dracula (U) Cary Grant (V) Rio Conchos (W) Lou Gossett (X) John G. Avildsen (Y) Picnic ('56) (Z) Rorke's Drift

46 The Players: Marlon Brando

(A) Omaha, Neb., April 3 1924 (B) Shattuck Military Academy (C) Erwin Piscator (D) The Man ('50) (E) Elia Kazan (F) The Teahouse of the August Moon ('56) (G) One Eyed Jacks, Rio (H) 1 Mark Antony 2 Johnny 3 Napoleon 4 Fletcher Christian 5 Don Corleone (I) Jocelyn Brando (J) Maria Schneider

47 The Movie Makers: Brigitte Bardot

(A) Roger Vadim (B) Le Trou Normand ('52) (C) Doctor at Sea ('56) (D) Juliette (E) Louis Malle

48 Screenplay

(A) Marlon Brando in On the Waterfront ('54) (B) James Stewart in The Philadelphia Story ('40) (C) Ali MacGraw in Love Story ('70) (D) John Wayne in The Searchers ('56) (E) Errol Flynn in The Adventures of Robin Hood ('38) (F) Paul Newman in Butch Cassidy and the Sundance Kid ('69) (G) Paul le Mat in American Graffiti ('73) (H) Humphrey Bogart in The Barefoot Contessa ('53) (I) Peter Sellers in Revenge of the Pink Panther ('78) (J) Strother Martin in Cool Hand Luke ('67)

49 The Movie Makers: Tony Curtis

(A) New York, June 3 1925 (B) Bernard Schwarz (C) Criss Cross ('48) (D) June 4 1951 (E) Albert de Salvo

50 Screen Test

(A) Michael Caine (B) Moe Howard, Larry Fine, Joe de Rita (C) Paris, April 27 1932 (D) Jerry Goldsmith (E) The Sting (F) Lee Marvin, Toshiro Mifune (G) The Tarriers (H) Michael Curtiz (I) The Special Edition (J) Alaska (K) Have Gun Will Travel, Paladin (L) Jenny Cavilleri

(M) Joan Plowright (N) 1 Jimmy Durante 2 Spencer Tracy 3 Terry Thomas 4 Dorothy Provine 5 Ethel Merman (O) 1967 (P) Jean Simmons & Donald Houston, Brooke Shields & Christopher Atkins (Q) Wesley Ruggles (R) Bo Widerberg (S) Maj. General Stanislaw Sosabowski (T) An auto-gyro (U) Hair styling (V) Mae West (W) 1 The Parent Trap ('61) 2 Pinocchio ('39) 3 Jungle Book ('67) 4 Peter Pan ('53) 5 The Monkey's Uncle ('64) (X) Once Is Not Enough ('75) (T) Christopher Lee (Z) Honor Blackman

51 The Players: James Dean

(A) Marion, Ind., February 8 1931 (B) James Byron Dean (C) Elia Kazan (D) Sailor Beware ('51) (E) Has Anybody Seen My Gal? ('51) (F) Samuel Fuller (G) See The Jaguar (H) Dick Davalos (I) Car accident, September 30 1955 (J) 1 Cal Trask 2 Jim Stark 3 Jett Rink

52 The Movie Makers: Sophia Loren

(A) Sophia Scicoloni (B) Cuori Sul Mare ('50) (C) Woman of the River ('55) (D) Carlo Ponti (E) Two Women

53 The Movie Makers: Jack Lemmon

(A) Boston, Mass., February 8 1925 (B) John Uther Lemmon III (C) It Should Happen To You ('53) (D) Days of Wine and Roses ('62) (E) Mister Roberts as Ensign Pulver, Save The Tiger as Harry Stoner

54 The Movie Makers: Peter Finch

(A) London, September 28 1916 (B) William Mitchell (C) Dad and Dave Come to Town ('37) (D) Sheriff of Nottingham (E) 1 Sunday Bloody Sunday ('71) 2 Father Brown ('54) 3 The Battle of the River Plate ('56) 4 The Trials of Oscar Wilde ('60) 5 Network ('76)

55 The Players: Elvis Presley

(A) Tupelo, Miss., January 8 1935 (B) Elvis Aaron Presley (C) Love Me Tender ('56) (D) Richard Thorpe (E) GI Blues ('60) (F) Marlon Brando

(G) Kid Galahad ('62) (H) Fun In Acapulco ('63) (I) Denis Sanders (J) 1 Change of Habit ('69) 2 Stay Away Joe ('68) 3 Charro ('69) 4 Loving You ('57) 5 Roustabout ('64)

56 The Movie Makers: Sidney Poitier

(A) Miami, Florida (B) No Way Out ('50) (C) The Blackboard Jungle ('55) (D) In the Heat of the Night ('67), They Call Me Mister Tibbs ('70), The Organization ('71) (E) Buck and the Preacher ('72)

57 The Movie Makers: James Garner

(A) James Baumgarner (B) Toward the Unknown ('56) (C) Hour of the Gun ('67) (D) Burt Kennedy (E) Maverick, Nichols, The Rockford Files

58 The Players: Audrey Hepburn

(A) Brussels, May 4 1929 (B) Audrey Hepburn-Ruston (C) One Wild Oat ('51) (D) Mel Ferrer (E) Roman Holiday ('53) (F) Sabrina ('54) (G) Natasha (H) Fred Zinnemann (I) Breakfast at Tiffany's ('61) (J) Albert Finney

59 Screen Test

(A) Joel Grey (B) Mervyn Le Roy (C) 1 The Twelve Chairs ('78) 2 Blazing Saddles ('74) 3 Young Frankenstein ('75) 4 High Anxiety ('78) 5 The Producers ('68) (D) James Brolin & Jill Clayburgh (E) Five Graves to Cairo ('43) (F) Tall Story ('60) (G) Marshal Simon Fry (H) Bob Baker (I) Somebody Up There Likes Me ('56) (J) Matt Helm (K) 1 Grover Cleveland 2 Lou Gehrig 3 Jim Piersall 4 Ben Hogan 5 Annette Kellerman (L) James Robertson Justice (M) Mikis Theodorakis (N) All have portrayed Sherlock Holmes (O) Flubber (P) 1925 (Q) Norman Foster (R) 1 Susannah York 2 Hugh Griffith 3 Edith Evans 4 Joan Greenwood 5 Albert Finney (S) William Berkeley Enos (T) Stephenson (U) The Family Way ('66), Twisted Nerve ('68), Endless Night ('72) (V) Aloha, Bobby and Rose (W) What's New Pussycat? ('65) (X) Alvah Bessie, Herbert

Biberman, Lester Cole, Edward Dmytryk, Ring Lardner Jr, John Howard Lawson, Albert Maltz, Sam Ornitz, Adrian Scott, Dalton Trumbo (Y) Richard Quine (Z) Athens

60 The Players: Paul Newman
(A) Cleveland, Ohio, January 26 1925 (B) New York Actors' Studio (C) The Silver Chalice ('54) (D) The Long Hot Summer ('58) (E) Robert Rossen (F) Rashomon ('51) (G) On the Harmfulness of Tobacco ('59) (H) WUSA ('70) (I) Slap Shot ('77) (J) 1 Until They Sail ('57) 2 The Left Handed Gun ('58) 3 Paris Blues ('61) 4 Hombre ('67) 5 The Sting ('73)

61 The Players: Steve McQueen
(A) Terence Steven McQueen (B) Herbert Berghof (C) The Blob (D) Josh Randell (E) St Louis (F) Card player (G) Nevada Smith ('66), Tom Horn ('79) (H) The Great Escape ('63) (I) Ali MacGraw (J) Ralph 'Papa' Thorson

62 The Movie Makers: Charles Bronson
(A) Charles Buchinski (B) Charles Laughton (C) Man with a Camera (D) 1 Kid Galahad ('62) 2 The Magnificent Seven ('60) 3 This Property Is Condemned ('66) (E) Michael Winner

63 The Movie Makers: James Coburn
(A) Ride Lonesome ('59) (B) Jeff Durain (C) Our Man Flint ('66), In Like Flint ('67) (D) The Rockford Files (E) Stephen Sondheim & Anthony Perkins

64 The Movie Makers: Michael Caine
(A) London, March 14 1933 (B) Maurice Micklewhite (C) A Hill In Korea ('56) (D) Terence Stamp (E) Harry Palmer

65 The Movie Makers: Peter O'Toole
(A) Connemara, August 2 1932 (B) Peter Seamus O'Toole (C) Kidnapped ('59) (D) Henry II (E) What's New Pussycat? ('65)

66 The Movie Makers: Sean Connery
(A) Edinburgh, August 25 1930 (B) Thomas Connery (C) No Road Back ('55) (D) Doctor No ('62) (E) Zed

67 Screen Test
(A) Walter Matasschanskayasky, Earthquake (B) 10.40 a.m. to noon (C) John Chambers (D) Title designer (E) Cold Turkey ('70) (F) Paul McCartney (G) 1 Wilfred Lawson 2 Alexander Davion 3 Nat King Cole 4 Robert Walker 5 Robert Alda (H) Auto racing (I) Anton Karas, zither (J) Bernard Herrmann (K) Laurence Naismith (L) Picnic ('56) (M) Karel Reisz (N) Max Fliescher (O) William Friese-Greene (P) De Forrest Kelley (Q) Audie Murphy (R) The Original Sin (S) $110,000 (T) 1 Charles Crichton 2 Julien Duvivier 3 Thorold Dickinson 4 A. Dovzhenko 5 George Cukor (U) Sandra Dee (V) Boldwood (W) Clark Gable (X) Madeline Kahn (Y) Boris Karloff (Z) Brian Keith

68 The Movie Makers: François Truffaut
(A) New Wave (B) 400 Blows ('59) (C) Jeanne Moreau (D) Best Foreign Film (E) Claude Lacombe

69 The Movie Makers: John Schlesinger
(A) Hampstead, London, February 16 1926 (B) Oxford (C) Black Legend (D) Midnight Cowboy ('69) (E) Julie Christie

70 The Players: Peter Sellers
(A) Southsea, Hants., September 8 1925 (B) Crazy People (C) Spike Milligan, Harry Secombe & Michael Bentine (D) Penny Points To Paradise ('51) (F) John & Roy Boulting (F) Mr Topaze (G) Three (H) A diamond (I) The Running, Jumping and Standing Still Film ('59) (J) Being There ('80)

71 The Players: Robert Redford
(A) Charles Robert Redford Jr (B) Santa Monica, Calif., August 18 1937 (C) Warhunt ('62) (D) The Chase ('66), Barefoot in the Park ('67), The Electric Horseman ('80) (E) Sydney Pollack (F) This Proper-

ty Is Condemned (G) Three (H) The Great Waldo Pepper, William Goldman & George Roy Hill (I) James Cagney (J) 1 Barefoot in the Park 2 The Hot Rock (UK How to Steal a Diamond) ('72) 3 Downhill Racer ('69) 4 The Candidate ('72) 5 The Electric Horseman

72 The Movie Makers: Dustin Hoffman
(A) Los Angeles, Calif., August 8 1937 (B) Madigan's Millions ('66) (C) Mike Nichols (D) Papillon ('73) (E) Roy Scheider

73 The Movie Makers: Gene Hackman
(A) San Bernadino, Calif. (B) Buck Barrow (C) Downhill Racer ('69) (D) Jerry Schatzberg (E) Twice, The French Connection ('71), French Connection II ('75)

74 The Movie Makers: George Segal
(A) New York City, February 13 1934 (B) The Young Doctors ('61) (C) Marion Sobol (D) Where's Poppa? ('70) (E) A Touch of Class ('73)

75 The Movie Makers: Woody Allen
(A) Brooklyn, New York, December 1 1935 (B) Allen Stewart Konigsberg (C) What's New Pussycat? ('65) (D) Four (E) Manhattan ('79)

76 The Players: Clint Eastwood
(A) Clinton Eastwood (B) San Francisco, Calif. May 31 1930 (C) Revenge of the Creature ('54) (D) Rowdy Yates (E) 1961, Sergio Leone (F) The Witches (le Streghe) (G) Hang 'Em High ('68) (H) Brian G. Hutton (I) Play Misty for Me ('71), Murphy (J) 1 The Beguiled ('71) 2 Kelly's Heroes ('70) 3 Paint Your Wagon ('69) 4 Dirty Harry ('71), Magnum Force ('73), The Enforcer ('77) 5 The Gauntlet ('78)

77 Screen Test
(A) D.W. Griffith (B) Tom Joad (C) Arthur Bliss (D) £227,000 (E) 1 S.M. Eisenstein 2 Nikolai Ekk 3 Oskar Fischinger 4 Fritz Lang 5 Garson Kanin & Carol Reed (F) Scarface

(G) Orson Welles as Citizen Kane (H) The Savage Innocents ('60) (I) 1 Richard Dreyfuss 2 Ronny Howard 3 Candy Clark 4 Paul le Mat 5 Cindy Williams (J) Peter O'Toole & Sian Phillips (K) Forty-two (L) Katy Jurado (M) The Third Day ('65) (N) Surfing (O) Victor McLaglen (P) Bonnie and Clyde (Q) Elizabeth Taylor, Michael Caine, Susannah York (R) Gina Lollobrigida (S) Anna Magnani (T) Eddie Foy Jr (U) Roy del Ruth (V) Modesty Blaise (W) The Honkers ('72) (X) Rape (Y) Gena Rowlands & Seymour Cassel (Z) Fuzz ('72)

78 The Players: Jack Nicholson

(A) Neptune, New Jersey, April 22 1937 (B) The Terror ('63) (C) The Monkees (D) The Trip ('67) (E) Easy Rider ('69) (F) Drive He Said ('70) (G) Warren Beatty & Stockard Channing (H) 1973 (I) The Missouri Breaks ('76) (J) Stanley Kubrick

79 The Players: Barbra Streisand

(A) Brooklyn, New York, April 24 1942 (B) Barbra Joan Streisand (C) Funny Girl ('68) (D) It was shared with Katharine Hepburn (E) Paul Newman, Sidney Poitier, Steve McQueen & Dustin Hoffman (F) George Segal (G) Katie Morosky (H) Peter Bogdanovich (I) Best Song – Evergreen (with Paul Williams) – from A Star is Born ('76) (J) Funny Lady ('75)

80 Screen Test

(A) Millicent Martin, Julia Foster, Shelley Winters, Jane Asher, Shirley Anne Field, Eleanor Bron, Viven Merchant (B) David Niven (C) Cavantina, Stanley Myers (D) Brigitte Bardot (E) Danny Kaye & Mel Brooks (F) George Richard Chamberlain (G) Cliff Robertson (H) William Asher (I) 1 Talia Shire 2 Burgess Meredith 3 Burt Young 4 Carl Weathers 5 Sylvester Stallone (J) Spanish (K) Jeffrey Hunter (L) Alfredo Pacino (M) Alistair Maclean (N) 1, 2, 3 & 5 Quincy Jones 4 Booker T. Jones (O) All have portrayed Gidget (P) Mario Lanza (Q) Lola Froblich (R) Fred Zinnemann

(S) Carl Laemmle (T) Uneasy Freehold (U) James MacArthur (V) Mel Blanc (W) All have portrayed Rasputin (X) Manhunt (Y) Mary Pickford (Z) The First of The Few

The Big Picture Quiz 1
King Kong

(A) 1933 (B) Edgar Wallace & Merian C. Cooper (C) Chief animator (D) Skull Island (E) Merian C. Cooper & Ernest B. Schoedsack (F) A ship (G) James A. Creelman & Ruth Rose (H) The Empire State Building, New York (I) 1 Robert Armstrong 2 Bruce Cabot 3 Fay Wray 4 Frank Reicher (J) 1976

The Big Picture Quiz 2
Gone with the Wind

(A) The Grand Theater, Atlanta, Georgia, December 15 1939 (B) David O. Selznick (C) Three, Victor Fleming, George Cukor & Sam Wood (D) Margaret Mitchell (E) Rhett Butler (F) Production designer (G) Sidney Howard (H) Rhett Butler (I) Nine (J) 1 Vivien Leigh 2 Leslie Howard 3 Olivia de Havilland 4 Thomas Mitchell 5 Hattie McDaniel

The Big Picture Quiz 3
Stagecoach

(A) 1939 (B) Ernest Haycox (C) John Ford (D) Richard Mageman, Frankie Harling, Louis Gruenberg, John Leipold, Leo Shuken (E) Dudley Nichols (F) Monument Valley, Arizona (G) Walter Wanger (H) 'The chase is too long' (I) 1966 (J) 1 Claire Trevor 2 Andy Devine 3 George Bancroft 4 Thomas Mitchell 5 John Wayne

The Big Picture Quiz 4
Casablanca

(A) 1943 (B) Murray Burnett & Joan Alison (C) Michael Curtiz (D) 1, 3 & 5 (E) Julius J. & Philip G. Epstein & Howard Koch (F) Paris (G) Action in the North Atlantic, Thank Your Lucky Stars & Sahara (H) Max Steiner (I) As Time Goes By, Herman Hupfield (J) 1 Humphrey Bogart 2 Claude Rains 3 Dooley Wilson 4 Ingrid Bergman 5 John Qualen

The Big Picture Quiz 5
Great Expectations

(A) 1946 (B) David Lean (C) Jaggers (D) Anthony Wager, Jean Simmons (E) Charles Dickens (F) Music score (G) Ronald Neame (H) Additional dialogue (I) Two, Guy Green – Best Black & White Cinematography, John Bryan & Wilfred Shingleton – Best Black & White Art Direction/Set Direction (J) 1 Alec Guinness 2 Bernard Miles 3 Finlay Currie 4 Martita Hunt 5 Hay Petrie

The Big Picture Quiz 6
From Here to Eternity

(A) 1953 (B) Fred Zinnemann (C) James Jones (D) Buddy Adler (E) Honolulu, Hawaii (F) Daniel Taradash (G) Hostess (H) Pearl Harbour (I) Eight, Buddy Adler – Best Film, Fred Zinnemann – Best Direction, Frank Sinatra – Best Supporting Actor, Donna Reed – Best Supporting Actress, Daniel Taradash – Best Screenplay, Burnett Guffey – Best Black & White Cinematography, John P. Livadary – Best Sound Recording, William Lyon – Best Editing (J) 1 Montgomery Clift 2 Burt Lancaster 3 Deborah Kerr 4 Frank Sinatra 5 Jack Warden

The Big Picture Quiz 7
Rebel without a Cause

(A) 1955 (B) Nicholas Ray (C) The Blind Run, Nicholas Ray (D) Irving Shulman (E) Sunset Boulevard ('50) (F) Stewart Stern (G) Plato (H) Leonard Rosenman (I) Producer (J) 1 Natalie Wood 2 Corey Allen 3 Ann Doran 4 Sal Mineo 5 Jim Backus

The Big Picture Quiz 8
King Creole

(A) 1958 (B) Michael Curtiz (C) Harold Robbins (D) A Stone for Danny Fisher (E) Hal Wallis (F) New Orleans (G) Jerry Leiber & Mike Stoller (H) Technical Adviser (I) Herbert Baker & Michael Vincente Gazzo (J) 1 Elvis Presley 2 Carolyn Jones 3 Walter Matthau 4 Vic Morrow 5 Dolores Hart

The Big Picture Quiz 9
West Side Story

(A) 1961 (B) Robert Wise & Jerome

Robbins (C) Leonard Bernstein (D) The Jets, The Sharks (E) Stephen Sondheim (F) Officer Krupke (G) Jerome Robbins (H) Ten (I) Ernest Lehman (J) 1 Natalie Wood 2 Richard Beymer 3 Russ Tamblyn 4 Rita Moreno 5 George Chakiris

The Big Picture Quiz 10
A Hard Day's Night
(A) 1964 (B) Richard Lester (C) Paul's Irish grandfather ('a very clean old man') (D) Alun Owen (E) Things We Said Today (F) Walter Shenson (G) Title artist (H) Patti Boyd (I) Lennon & McCartney (J) John Lennon, Paul McCartney, George Harrison, Ringo Starr

The Big Picture Quiz 11
Guess Who's Coming to Dinner
(A) 1967 (B) Stanley Kramer (C) John Prentice (D) William Rose (E) San Francisco, Calif. (F) Stanley Kramer (G) The Glory of Love (H) Two, Katharine Hepburn – Best Actress, William Rose – Best Story & Screenplay (I) Postman (J) 1 Katharine Hepburn 2 Spencer Tracy 3 Katharine Houghton 4 Beah Richards 5 Cecil Kellaway

The Big Picture Quiz 12
Butch Cassidy and the Sundance Kid
(A) 1969 (B) William Goldman (C) George Roy Hill (D) The Union Pacific Flyer (E) Salt Lake Herald (F) Burt Bacharach (G) Bolivia (H) B.J. Thomas (I) Downhill Racer, Tell Them Willie Boy Is Here, Winning (J) 1 Paul Newman 2 Robert Redford 3 Katharine Ross 4 Strother Martin 5 Cloris Leachman

The Big Picture Quiz 13
Midnight Cowboy
(A) 1969 (B) John Schlesinger (C) James Leo Herlihy (D) Fred Neil (E) Elephants Memory, The Groop (F) Waldo Salt (G) He sang 'Everybody's Talkin'' (H) Three, Jerome Hellman – Best Film (producer), John Schlesinger – Best Direction, Waldo Salt – Best Screenplay (I) Jerome Hellman (J) 1 Jon Voight 2 Sylvia Miles 3 John McGiver 4 Brenda Vaccaro 5 Dustin Hoffman

The Big Picture Quiz 14
One Flew Over the Cuckoo's Nest
(A) 1975 (B) Ken Kesey (C) Milos Forman (D) Five (E) Lawrence Hauben & Bo Goldman (F) Charmaine (G) Haskell Wexler (H) Saxophone solo in 'Call of the West' (I) Jack Nitzche (J) 1 William Redfield 2 Louise Fletcher 3 Will Sampson 4 Scatman Crothers 5 Jack Nicholson

The Big Picture Quiz 15
Jaws
(A) 1975 (B) Steven Spielberg (C) Peter Benchley (D) Martha's Vineyard, Mass. (E) Original music score (F) Peter Benchley & Carl Gottlieb (G) Amity (H) 1 Roy Scheider 2 Murray Hamilton 3 Richard Dreyfuss 4 Robert Shaw 5 Lorraine Gary (I) The Great White Shark (J) Jaws II

Mystery Stars
(1) Cyd Charisse (2) Broderick Crawford (3) Charles Boyer (4) Richard Dreyfuss (5) Faye Dunaway (6) Buster Keaton (7) Jane Wyman (8) Mae West (9) Alan Ladd (10) Roddy McDowall (11) Candice Bergen (12) Fernando Lamas (13) Joan Crawford (14) Janet Leigh (15) Roy Rogers (16) Marlene Dietrich (17) Vincent Price (18) Bette Davis (19) Grace Kelly (20) Melvyn Douglas (21) Claudette Colbert (22) Marion Davies

Film Posters
(1) Hearts of the World ('18) (2) The Magic Flame ('27) (3) Porgy and Bess ('59) (4) Hey There It's Yogi Bear ('65) (5) The Pink Panther ('63)

Star Couples
(1) Charles Bronson & Jill Ireland (2) Steve McQueen & Ali MacGraw (3) Bobby Darin & Sandra Dee (4) Paul Newman & Joanne Woodward (5) Richard Burton & Elizabeth Taylor (6) Robert Taylor & Barbara Stanwyck (7) Mell Ferrer & Audrey Hepburn (8) Tony Curtis & Janet Leigh (9) Clark Gable & Carole Lombard (10) Humphrey Bogart & Lauren Bacall

About the author
Cardiff born graphic designer **Rob Burt** has specialised in chronicling the popular arts. He has compiled and designed and written sleeve notes for many rock, jazz and movie soundtrack albums. His books include: *The Beatles: The Fabulous Story of John, Paul, George and Ringo*, *The West Coast Story* and *The Illustrated Rock Quiz*.

A recognised *land surfer* he lives in West London with his wife and two children. Among his influences he lists Fairwater, Lawrence Sweet, John Arvanities, Jeremy Pascall, Derek Taylor, Charlie Byrd, Earl Klugh, Claude Lelouch, Charles Webster, Stan Getz and James Garner.

Acknowledgements
The author gratefully acknowledges the help of Sarah Harman, Peter Campbell, Robin Wood, Rosemary Goodfriend, Stewart Cowley, Diana Levinson, Cinema International Corporation, Columbia EMI Warner, Fantasy Films, United Artists, Walt Disney Productions, The Stills Library – British Film Institute and Kirk Douglas.

The photograph of Barry Norman on page 3 is BBC copyright.

Special thanks to Lizzie Burt